AF254970

Jesus Savior of All

Jesus Savior of All

DENBURK GREGORY

Copyright © 2020 by Denburk Gregory.

Library of Congress Control Number: 2020923877

HARDBACK: 978-1-953791-59-7
PAPERBACK: 978-1-953791-58-0
EBOOK: 978-1-953791-60-3

All rights reserved. No part of this publication may be reproduced, distributed, or transmitted in any form or by any electronic or mechanical means, without the prior written permission of the publisher, except in the case of brief quotations embodied in critical reviews and certain other noncommercial uses permitted by copyright law.

Ordering Information:

For orders and inquiries, please contact:
1-888-404-1388
www.goldtouchpress.com
book.orders@goldtouchpress.com

Printed in the United States of America

CONTENTS

DEDICATION

On behalf of my siblings and me, we would like to take this moment to recognize our sweet darling grandmother, Sister Vera Thomas (granny mama), who has passed away a long time now. However, we still remember her as if she was still alive today because she grew us up with love and care, but most importantly, in the knowledge of the fear of the Lord God.

We remember every Sunday morning without any excuses that we must be ready for Sunday school, and later, she would join us for Sunday morning service. After Sunday morning service, we would walk home and eat dinner and then get ourselves ready again for the night service. Our grandmother was a sweet, kind-hearted person in our neighborhood, and we never experienced her quarreling with another person. I remember when our grandmother would sit with us and tell us stories of the past, and it makes us laugh as we listen. Our grandmother was strict because of who she was and who she belongs to, and she tries her very best to instill those qualities in us. We grew up in a loving and God-fearing home, and it certainly makes a big difference in our lives, even now as adults.

Our life with granny mama was a terrific and very peaceful period of our life as we grew from a babe to an adult under her care. There is so much more to complement our grandmother for, but this is not the time. We did indeed love our granny mama, and we still love you even though you are not present in the body.

Our grandmother never once put up with our nonsense because she was the parent, and we were the children. As we were growing up under her care, we were trained to be respectful to self, to her, and others just because she was the adult and guardian, and we were the children; respect was to be given to the adult in those days, whether at home or on the street. It is not like now when children are doing whatever they please and disrespecting their parents, grandparents, and strangers.

Children and grandchildren, what many of you are doing now to your parents and the older ones among you is not right, and it certainly does not please God who holds our lives into His precious hands.

We remember many good times, yet for me, the writer, sometimes I cry within my heart when I remember what I have heard about the last few years of my grandmother's life upon this earth; the way she was treated, not by strangers but by family members. May God have mercy upon the souls of those who abuse the elderly; then again, maybe they did not know how to care for her at her age. We have to very careful how we treat the older ones among us because one day, we may reap what we have sown. Granny mama, I know that you cannot hear us, your grandchildren, but for the times when we cause you to talk to us over and over about the same things, please, Father God, forgive us. When we disobey you by not following your godly instruction, again, Father God, forgive us.

Grandmother (granny mama), we love you dearly, and we are so sorry that we were not there for you when you needed us the most as you were there for us when we were a child and needed you the most. We know that you cannot hear or respond to us because of where you are, but by God's grace, we shall meet again in God's heavenly Kingdom if we live our lives as you have lived yours for Jesus Christ, the Son of the Highest God, our Father. Until then, grandmother, enjoy your rest in Jesus.

Your grandchildren and their family.

APPRECIATION

To my darling wife, Veronica Gregory, I just want to express to you in writing that I truly appreciate you for all the things you have done for me. You are the queen of my life, and I love you. Thank you for those times you had to put up with me all these years during our marriage. There have been some ups and downs, yes; there were valleys, but thank God in Jesus' name that He kept us alive and well for a time that is coming very soon when the Lord will have us experience the mountain top experience, both spiritual and the natural things of this world.

Please, my wife, I encourage you to continue to live for Jesus because he loves you more than I love you, and He cares for you more than I do. Also, when I may disappoint you, Jesus Christ will never let you down.

And I know that one day by God's extraordinary grace, He will bless me so that you can experience the mountain top experience while alive. It is my wish that the Lord God will bless me so that I can show you kindness in ways that you would not believe, but by the grace of almighty God, it shall come to pass. As you are blessed, I pray that you will, in turn, be a blessing to others so that our God, and Father in heaven, and His Son, Jesus Christ, will get glory from our lives.

To God be all the glory. Many thanks, my darling wife, for all your support in every area of my life. Thank you for your help in the ministry that the Lord Jesus Christ has called us into for Himself. You have pushed me to be a better person and encourage me to be successful in whatever state I find myself in. I remember how you helped me to take a promotion that I did not want, and now I am so glad that I listened to you. I also thank my coworker, Ms. Kitty, who was an instrument of this promotion through her encouragement.

I appreciate you very much and again, many, many thanks. Also, thank you for your kindness to our children as a parent in Jesus' precious name.

Your husband,
Denburk Gregory

CHILDREN

With a sincere heart, we would like to extend a warm thank you to our children who stood by us even when things were sometimes not perfect. We also ask for your forgiveness for anything that we may have said or done in haste. Children, please remember what we were able to do for each of you was because of Almighty God and His Son, Jesus Christ, who helped us. Also, please remember, children, the best decision that anyone of you could make in your entire life is for each of you to surrender your life to Jesus and make Him your Lord and Savior. God bless each of you in Jesus' precious and holy name. Once again, children, don't forget that without Jesus Christ, you cannot enter into the Kingdom of heaven, so please surrender your life to Him.

Many thanks and lots of love,
Dad & Mom

ACKNOWLEDGMENTS

I would like to recognize our Bishop, Bishop Arthur Brown, and his wife, Pastor Beverly Brown, for the work they have been doing for the Lord God and His Son Jesus Christ. Thank you so much for showing us kindness and your support in the opening of the **Full Truth Church of God Deliverance Center in Cumming, Georgia.** We have come to see that the fruit of the Spirit is your daily living.

Many thanks to our church families in Kingston, Jamaica, Toronto, Canada, Bronx, New York, and Florida, not forgetting Georgia.

Again, Bishop Brown, we appreciate you for you and the Christ that is in you. Continue to do the work of the Lord, and He will reward on that particular day that is coming.

Pastor Gregory
&
Minister Veronica

Romans 9:1 (KJV) tells us: "I say the truth in Christ, I lie not, my conscience also bearing me witness in the Holy Ghost,"

I am delighted to say this, as the Apostle Paul. I lie not concerning the information in this book. The purpose of this book is to help my brothers and sisters in Christ to arise from their sleep and be on fire for Jesus Christ. He is the One who died for our sins and the only one who shed His precious blood for us, and He has within Himself Eternal life. No human being can possess this life, and no human being has this life, only Jesus Christ of Nazareth, the Son of the Virgin Mary as a man that walks this earth can give us this life. The scripture below tells us of such.

Besides Jesus Christ, there is no other Savior that our Father God has sent into this world to save humanity from their sins, and there will be no other because there is no end to His reign. Jesus Christ is the king of all kings and the Lord of all lords. **Amen.**

John 5:26 (KJV)
[26] For as the Father hath life in himself; so hath he given to the Son to have life in himself;

This book is to help those who are struggling in their faith in God, not knowing who the Father and the Son, Jesus Christ, indeed are. Many people have been mixing them up to be one person with three different personalities. In this book, you will get information that will help you in your walk with the Lord, and many other denominations will be blessed from this writing if you are teachable. As you read this book, you will need The Holy Bible to see what the full content of the scripture references is telling you. The Bible contained vital information for our learning; however, sometimes, you will need to read a few verses above or after to get a better understanding of that particular verse that we bring forth to you for discussion. Remember this: this book is not about the writer; it is all about the Father, Son, and Holy Ghost. I am just a vessel who avails myself to the Lord so that He can do whatsoever He chooses to do with this vessel. I pray to God in heaven that the pastors will stop preaching compromising messages that some have been preaching while people are dying and going to hell. The Lord God is the one who employed you to do His work for Him in this earth and not man; therefore, stop pleasing humanity and do the work that you were called to do by the Almighty God which art in heaven.

Were you not called into this profession to teach or preach the living and written Word? Many Christians do not understand the word of God as they need to. Therefore, God put us, His servants, those that He called to work in His Kingdom or Vineyard to teach them. Christians are not reading the word of God as they should, and many Christians are not praying as they should. I write to you to encourage everyone, both Christians and unbelievers, that Jesus is the only One who can save us from our sins. Therefore, we need to put our trust only in Him, because He is the only one that has made promises to us and never one time fail to keep any of His promises. When He said that He would never leave us nor forsake us, Jesus meant every word that was spoken.

My prayers are that all of us will come to the knowledge and revelation of the Lord Jesus Christ and begin to be on fire for our King. Sinners, hell is real, and I encourage you to give your life unto the Lord Jesus Christ today so that He can save you from your sins. Know this, there is no one else that can do such except Jesus, this is the plan that God the Father has set up, and we cannot change it; therefore, let us accept Him and move on in the things of the Almighty God.

Thank you, readers, for purchasing this book. Because you have, you are helping so many people in ways that you do not know. Some of the proceeds are to support the building of our church building where people can come and give their life to Jesus, where people can go and receive deliverance from the oppression of the devil, and where people can come to be prayed for and see Jesus Christ manifest Himself under the anointing of the Holy Spirit and demons will flee in Jesus' name and receive of the Father blessing from above. At our church and many others, I pray that we will remember the One that called us into this profession and the reason why we were assigned this task. As we reflect, let all the servants of the living God that are called by His holy name continue to preach and teach the word of truth without compromising the truth to please people. Children of God, we will pray for you and with you to live a victorious life in the only begotten Son of God holy name.

We will pray for the unsaved that they, too, will come to know Jesus Christ as their Savior because, without the Son of God, there is no hope for humanity. Let us obey God so that we can enter into His rest on judgment day. Therefore, unsaved ones, please examine your life now and what it will be after you die. Will you reign with Christ forever, or will you be separated from Him forever?

Children of God, do not let Jesus come back and leave you behind; this is for the lukewarm Christians. Judge yourself and see if your life is what God said it should be and, if not, repent of your sins and correct your mistakes so that you will be found faultless according to the word of God. Sinners, you have been putting off the call to repentance for your life for too long now; it is time for you to take that step of boldness and call out to God to save you in the only name that is above every name in this entire earth, yes, there is no name like this name, Jesus. Who is that? Jesus. What is His name again? Jesus. Only Jesus Christ can deliver us from the wrath of God that is coming, and the only escape is to accept Him as your Lord and savior.

We, the people of the earth, are experiencing something that we have never experienced before now, and that something has affected people's lives. Many business places closed; many have closed and may not able to open again because of the financial damage that this virus causes. Because of the seriousness of this virus that is called Coronavirus

(Covid19), even churches were closed and could not open to preach the word of God because of the restriction, however, this is where people can come to find refuge in Jesus. It is regrettable that the entire earth, all at once, is going through this terrible ordeal, and there is no immediate help for humanity except Jesus. Still, we need to trust God in this matter and take all the precautions that are expected of us for our families and neighbors to be safe in Jesus' name.

In April of 2018, the **Full Truth Church of God Deliverance Center,** Head Quarter in Kingston, Jamaica W.I., conducted the annual church convention under the leadership of Bishop Arthur Brown, and God gave him the theme for the convention, a very profound topic. The Theme was *"Spiritual Immunization Against Diabolical Diseases."* Have you gotten your spiritual vaccine as yet? The vaccine is the precious blood of Jesus Christ.

This disease and plague that has caused much death and health uncertainty has turned people's lives upside down, and fear has caused many to be in their prison. Satan, our enemy, wants us to live in fear; we rebuke this spirit of fear from this country and the world in Jesus' name. We, the people throughout the entire earth, must acknowledge that we need a spiritual immunization from the Lord Jesus by the Holy Spirit against the diseases and attack from demons that have come upon the world. It is not all about this virus; instead, it is about every Satanic activity in the lives of people. While we are waiting for the development of vaccines, let us seek the face of the Lord God in prayer, and you are encouraged to read **Psalm 91** and decree it upon your family, also, **2ⁿᵈ Chronicles 7:13-15.**

This experience that all of us are going through, the Lord will see us through, and we will survive it in Jesus' name. This virus has caused families to spend more time with each other because of the quarantine that was in place. However, it is unfortunate of the adverse reports that I have heard that some families are not getting along with each other.

This time of uncertainty and stressful period that we are facing, we should be more kind and loving to each other, but now, many of us are doing the opposite. After the virus is no more, what will our life be? Will we go back to our old ways, hating and disrespecting others? Or, will we start loving one another as Jesus already commanded all of us to do? Many Christian are living in fear which is of Satan, God the Lord did not give His children the spirit of fear. So why are you so fearful?

I am not saying that the Lord sent this virus/plague upon the earth, but He allowed it to happen. Nevertheless, do we see the Lord in this, or do we hear Him speaking to all of us? Nothing happens without the knowledge of the Lord; again, He allowed it to be. Let us all draw closer to God by repenting of our sins and worship Him who has all knowledge of things to come. Family and friends, neighbors and coworkers, learn something from this experience. Let us not wait for trouble to enter our home or Nation before we remember that we did not pray—pray without ceasing according to the word of God, **1ˢᵗ Thessalonians 5:17,** but how many of us are calling on the name of Jesus Christ for help? Everybody is looking for something or someone to put their trust in so that their mind will be at ease, but Jesus can help. Except for those who are genuinely grounded in Jesus know what to do.

Things are upside down as we speak, whether here or there, fear has become food for many because they don't know who Jesus is. People are troubled and anxiety has overtaken many because they have not yet anchored on the solid Rock, and I am not speaking of the natural stone; instead, this Solid Rock is Jesus Christ. Fear has entered the hearts and minds of people and they have nowhere to run to, but I know of a place that we can hide under the shadow of the Almighty God. **Psalm 91:1.** Have you gotten your vaccination as yet from Jesus, which is His blood?

When Satan uses people to disrupt your life, God and His Son, Jesus Christ, will stable you only if you will let them come into your life and home. When they come in and taken up residence, the devils will have to flee. To all nations, we are not calling on Jesus Christ as we need to; instead, we are looking at other places and people for help when God already has the answers for your life and condition before the foundation of the earth. Yes, the Lord will use people to be a blessing, and He used people to help you, but without Him, they could not do anything anyway; therefore, all of our help is in the Lord Jesus and not in human beings. **"Trust God and live."**

The scripture said this,

Psalm 121:1-4 (KJV)
[1] I will lift up mine eyes unto the hills, from whence cometh my help.
[2] My help *cometh* from the LORD, which made heaven and earth.
[3] He will not suffer thy foot to be moved: he that keepeth thee will not slumber.
[4] Behold, he that keepeth Israel shall neither slumber nor sleep.

What the Lord is saying to us here on earth is put your trust in Him and not man, man will fail you, but I the Lord will not fail you?

CHAPTER ONE

Worship and praise

The Spirit of God spoke to us clearly and said this in the book of Revelation.

Revelation 3:22 (KJV)
22 He that hath an ear, let him hear what the Spirit saith unto the churches.

Hear ye nations of the earth, from the four corners; those who have an ear to hear, hear the word of God because He is speaking by calling us to attention. No matter if you are high or low, rich or poor, know this for surety, all power belongs to the Lord, the Almighty God, and He is in control from heaven to earth.

Psalm 62:11-12 (KJV)
11 God hath spoken once; twice have I heard this; that power *belongeth* unto God.
12 Also unto thee, O Lord, *belongeth* mercy: for thou renderest to every man according to his work.

Hear this, all ye people, give ear all ye inhabitants of the world, all power belongeth unto God.

Father God, we come to you as humble as we know how in the mighty name of your Son Jesus. Father, we commit ourselves unto you by surrendering our lives into your hands. Father God, forgive us of our sins that we have committed against Thee because it is you, and you alone, we have sinned against. Search our hearts, oh God, and see if there is any wicked ways in us, and cleanse us from all unrighteousness in Jesus' name.

Psalms 51:7 (KJV)

[7] Purge me with hyssop, and I shall be clean: wash me, and I shall be whiter than snow.

Create in us a clean heart, oh God, and renew a right spirit within us, we pray in Jesus name. We also pray, dear Lord, that you will cover our mind with the precious blood of Jesus. Father, we have chosen to forgive all those who have used and abused us for profits. All those who have offended us and done us wrong in Jesus' name.

Matthew 6:14-15 (KJV)

[14] For if ye forgive men their trespasses, your heavenly Father will also forgive you:
[15] But if ye forgive not men their trespasses, neither will your Father forgive your trespasses.

Father God, we worship you because you are the only true and living God that there is and should be worshipped. We praise you and honor you. You are the Sovereign Lord. It is you, oh God, who has created the heavens, the earth and the sea, and all that is in them. Oh LORD God, you are the One who rules the whole "Universe," and you are the Father of all humanity.

We worship you in spirit and truth; at your feet only, we bow down and surrender ourselves unto Thee. There is no other God in the heaven of heavens besides thee; neither is there anyone on this earth that is like unto you. Who is like unto you, Oh God? There is none. Father, throughout the entire world from the four corners of the earth, I have not known any that is like Thee; therefore, we give you all the honor, glory, and praise. There is no one or anything, whether seen or unseen, that is above you. Heaven is your throne, and the earth is your footstool.

Acts 7:49-50 (KJV)

49 Heaven *is* my throne, and earth *is* my footstool: what house will ye build me? saith the Lord: or what *is* the place of my rest?
50 Hath not my hand made all these things?

We praise thee, Oh God, for who you are, and with a heart of thanksgiving, we thank you for all the blessings upon our lives. Lord, not only for those who are called by your holy name but also for those who haven't yet accepted you.

Oh LORD God, you are holy, you are so holy Lord, and there is no other but you. There are so many things that you have created, and many are using them as gods; forgive them, dear Lord, in Jesus' name. All those things are not like you; you are more excellent. In ignorance, many of us sin against you because we do not know You as we should, You are the only true and living God that there is. Many worship that which they have no real knowledge of, and they are a follower of destruction. But those that know you worship thee only. Jehovah God, you are Awesome. You are a mighty God, and you are from everlasting to everlasting, and you are God. Yes, Lord Jesus, we love you because you first loved us.

Yes, Father, we accept Jesus Christ as your only-begotten Son, and He is the Lamb of the only true and living God. Yes, Lord Jesus, we thank you for coming into this wicked and sinful world to be the perfect sacrifice for humanity. Lord Jesus, thank you for shedding your blood for us so that our heavenly Father can forgive our sins. You are worthy of being praised; there is no other that deserves the praises that are due unto your holy and precious name. Lord, from the rising of the sun, unto the going down of the very same, Father God, you are worthy to be praised.

Yes, Father, You have given back to us the authority that was taken from us by Satan, and now we have power over the works of the enemy only in the name of Jesus Christ of Nazareth.

Mark 16:15-18 (KJV)

[15] And he said unto them, Go ye into all the world, and preach the gospel to every creature.

[16] He that believeth and is baptized shall be saved; but he that believeth not shall be damned.

[17] And these signs shall follow them that believe; In my name shall they cast out devils; they shall speak with new tongues;

[18] They shall take up serpents; and if they drink any deadly thing, it shall not hurt them; they shall lay hands on the sick, and they shall recover.

Prayer of Warfare and Deliverance against the enemy:

1. In the mighty name of Jesus, I cancel every evil work that the devil has planned against my family and me.

2. I renounce every evil covenant, conscious or unconscious, that I have entered into in the name of Jesus.

3. I up-root every corrupted tree that was planted in the lives of my family in the name of Jesus.

4. I bind every demonic activity in my home, in the life of my (husband, wife, children, and grandchildren) in the name of Jesus.

5. I call upon the fire of the Holy Ghost to consume and burn up every demonic residue in us and around us.

6. In the mighty name of Jesus, I come against every satanic activity in my church. Lord Jesus, cleanse your servants from any evil doings with your precious blood.

7. We release ourselves from the bondage of demonic oppression, depression, sicknesses, diseases, and premature death, in the mighty name of Jesus.

8. I command you, devils, to lose your grip from off my (husband, wife, children, and grandchildren) in the mighty name of Jesus.

9. Father God, I pray that you will protect my (husband, wife, children, and grandchildren) mind against the attack of the enemy. We understand that the enemy comes to steal, kill, and to destroy us, but we ask of you, Oh Lord, cover our mind with the blood of Jesus.

10. Father preserve our mind even at an old age so that we will be able to function with all of our senses, knowing how to continue serving you in worship, praising you, honor and thanksgiving, and giving you all the glory in Jesus' name.

11. Father God, I bind the spirit of Sodom and Gomorrah from our children. Lord, I pray that none of the ungodly acts of those cities will come upon our children and grandchildren's lives, even their children, children.

12. We bind the spirit of Baal from out of our homes, and we command you to take your filthy hands from off our finances in the mighty name of Jesus.

13. We cancel any covenant that we have entered into with Baal through ignorance in Jesus' name.

14. Father God, there are so many diseases and sicknesses that are destroying the lives of many of your children. Lord Jesus, you said that by your stripe, we are healed; therefore, we pray that you will heal them to the glory of God.

15. Father God, we declare the blood of Jesus upon our pastor's life in the mighty name of Jesus Christ. We also ask for a cleansing of the pulpit in Jesus' name. Purge the church from sin, sweet Jesus, so that our Father in heaven will be glorified in the church and so that you also will be glorified by the Father in us and through us.

16. Every weapon that forms against our church, pastor/s, and the children of God shall not prosper in Jesus' name, and every tongue that rises against us according to your word, let them be condemned in Jesus name.

17. Every weapon that forms against my (husband, wife, children, and grandchildren) shall not prosper, and every tongue that rises against us, oh God, according to your word, let them be condemned in Jesus mighty name.

18. Father God, we call upon your angels to come and surround us and protect us against the strong man against our life. Your word said that they are your ministering spirit; therefore, Lord, send them to come and minister to us, your people in this earth, in Jesus' name.

19. Father, in the mighty name of Jesus, we bind the spirit behind the diseases that are attacking some of your children. Father God, your word said that by your stripe, we were healed; therefore, we claim our healing by faith because our sickness and diseases were nailed to the cross.

*20. Father God, in the mighty name of Jesus Christ, we take authority over cancer. We command cancer to dry up and leave the body of my family **(call out the person's name that is sick).***

21. Father God, we come against diabetes in the mighty name of Jesus, and we ask that you will touch and heal with thy power.

Holy Spirit, whatever it is that we need to pray for that we do not know how to, we ask that you will intervene and travail on our behalf. Lord Jesus, thank you that you are on the right hand of the Father making intercession on our behalf. Therefore, even right now, please make petitions on behalf of our children and their families. Father God, we thank you for hearing and answering our prayers in Jesus' name.

Heavenly Father, we thank you for your Son Jesus, who died for our sins, who shed His precious blood on the cross at Calvary. We thank you for His death, His burial, and His resurrection. We thank you, Oh

God, that you have forgiven the sins of all those who accepted the call to repentance to receive forgiveness of our sins. We thank you for the blood of Jesus that washes and cleanses us from all unrighteousness.

Oh Lord God, we pray that you will give us the strength that we will need to love you, as the scripture has said.

Deuteronomy 6:5 (KJV)
5 And thou shalt love the LORD thy God with all thine heart, and with all thy soul, and with all thy might.

Matthew 22:37 (KJV)
37 Jesus said unto him, Thou shalt love the Lord thy God with all thy heart, and with all thy soul, and with all thy mind.

Luke 10:27 (KJV)
27 And he answering said, Thou shalt love the Lord thy God with all thy heart, and with all thy soul, and with all thy strength, and with all thy mind; and thy neighbour as thyself.

Father God, help us as human beings that we will learn to love our neighbors as you have commanded us to do. Father, how can we love if there is no love within us; therefore, we ask that you will fill our hearts with your divine love. Your pure love in our hearts we do need. Teach us how to love one another regardless of who they are or where they may come from, whether they are rich or poor—we all belong to You. Father, we want the love of Jesus, your Son, to abide in us continually for your glory.

Father, forever shall we praise you. Oh Lord, we glorify your precious name; there is no one like unto you, Lord. We love you and adore you. Lord, our soul cries out unto Thee for help; therefore, help us, we pray. Jesus, fill us with your love; let your love become liquid and flow throughout our entire body.

Oh LORD God, teach us how to worship you like the beast and the elders worship you as mentioned in ***Revelation 4:8-11.*** All your children desire to worship you, with true worship, dear Lord, we pray. So come, and even now, come and minister to us so that we can all please you.

Father God, it is not about us, it is all about your Son, Jesus Christ, who died for our sins, and we thank you and praise you for our salvation in Jesus' name. Oh, glory hallelujah to your holy name. Oh LORD God, we all thank you for your Holy Spirit, who dwells within us, He who is our Comforter and Teacher of the Living and written Word. We thank you for the power of your Holy Spirit, which has and still is working in the lives of our children.

We praise you and honor you, and we love you very, very much. To God be the glory, ***AMEN!***

CHAPTER TWO

Who are GOD and the Son?

From everlasting to everlasting, Jehovah God is God. He is the true GOD, and there is no other throughout the entire Universe besides Him.

Psalms 90:1-2 (KJV)
¹ Lord, thou hast been our dwelling place in all generations.
² Before the mountains were brought forth, or ever thou hadst formed the earth and the world, even from everlasting to everlasting, thou *art* God.

Isaiah 43:10 (KJV)
¹⁰ Ye *are* my witnesses, saith the LORD, and my servant whom I have chosen: that ye may know and believe me, and understand that I *am* he: before me there was no God formed, neither shall there be after me.

In the beginning, "the dateless past" Jehovah God, the LORD God Almighty, the Sovereign One, who is from everlasting to everlasting, came forth of Himself. We will never come to the understanding of everything about the LORD because we are not able to comprehend all of His wisdom, knowledge, and glory, **Deuteronomy 29:29**. However, what we need to do is to believe God by faith that the words that are written in **The Holy Bible** are right, **Hebrews 11:6.** All the words of the LORD God that came forth from His mouth are true because God is not a man that He should lie, and not one word will go back unto

Him without accomplishing that which He has sent it forth to do, and the word of God is inspired by the Holy Spirit of God and given to man to write.

The LORD God is the self-existent One; He came forth of Himself, that is why the Lord is God, and nothing or no one is before Him because He is from everlasting to everlasting. If there were other things or any humankind that exists before GOD, they would be God, because they would have been before the Almighty. Again, there is nothing or no one that was before GOD, and that's why He is GOD, and He will ever be God.

Jesus Christ is the Son of the living God, and He is before all things. The Holy Spirit, He too is before all things, and He is the Spirit of God, and the three make up the God-head, which is also referred to as the Trinity. The mind of mankind cannot contain the Wisdom of God or His Knowledge; therefore, we are to study His word (**The Holy Bible**) and believe by faith (acting on the promises of God) that what the scripture said about the Father, the Son, and the Holy Ghost is all true.

When God speaks, all things that He commanded come forth into existence by His Son, Jesus Christ. Too many people do not understand the creation of the universe and the existence of mankind and all other things visible or invisible; therefore, because they have no knowledge of God, they did not give God the glory, instead they came up with a rationale answer. But by faith, most of humanity believed that God created the heavens and the earth and everything that is in them. Because of pride in the heart of humanity, they would instead take the credit for the work of another. Even now, some people still refuse to acknowledge that it was Jehovah God who made the Universe, and they do not want to give the LORD God, the self-existent One, the honor and glory for His Creations. What happened is that many are in the position of influence, and they make their report of rationality to justify the creations of the Universe, including the existence of humanity and other things. However, by doing so, they have stolen the honor and praise that belongs to the Creator, God. They took the recognition for themselves to make themselves to be someone that they are not, concerning the creation of the Universe and all that there is in it. God alone is to be praised for The excellent work of His hands.

In ignorance, we lack true knowledge or presumptuousness, and we have been teaching the generations throughout the world of evolution. Yes, this earth is changing, and it is not a surprise to the Almighty God. Before the creation of the universe, the LORD, the God of all knowledge, knew all the things that we would do to pollute the earth because the heart of man is full of wickedness, and they become reckless towards one to another. Within our hearts lieth hate, death, and destruction of the planet earth to a degree and humanity. We all need Jesus, the Savior of humanity, to deliver us from the wrath to come.

All that is going on in this world is not a surprise to the Almighty God. However, as a loving and caring God and Father of all of us, He put in place things that must happen to cleanse this earth from mankind's selfishness and greed. Therefore, we don't need to panic as humans cannot destroy the planet earth; if it were possible that humans could destroy the earth, God word would not be accurate concerning His promises.

This world did not come from a big bang theory, as many believe—and thank God, it is just humanity's theory. However, it is high time for all of us to give the Lord, Jehovah God, all the praise, honor, and glory for His creation of the Universe. This present world is a restoration from the original creation that God created, but something terrible happened: sin manifested itself by Satan. Many do not know this truth, yet the facts are written and contained in the Holy Bible. So, what God did was restore this present world from its voided state, as mentioned in Genesis Chapter one, verse two. As you continue to read on in the book of Genesis, you will see where God restores the earth to a perfect form again until Satan deceives Adam and Eve and sin manifests itself again. Because of sin through the disobedience of humanity, the world is facing climatic changes and civil unrest throughout the earth. While many are addressing climate changes and the lack of two parents' in the homes, we are busy blaming this one and that one, forgetting to focus on the main reason for our problems, which is sin in our lives. A father not being at home to help raise his children in the right and proper way should not be an excuse for a child to do wrong. What about the home where there is no male figure present and still the children turn out to be a superstar. Until now, in many homes with available parents, some of the children are still brutish. It is not about who is present or absent; it is the condition of that individual hearts, whether the love of God in there or not. Always, the presence of God is Peace; the absence of God is Satan, which is no peace.

In heaven, angels are worshipping God and giving Him all glory and honor unto the Lord because the Lord is God. Why aren't we giving Him the glory, honor, and praise because He gave His life for our lives? God sent His Son, Jesus, to die for mankind's sin; therefore, all of us need to bow at the feet of Jehovah God and worship Him, honor Him and praise Him for what He has done for us. There was no need for Jesus to shed His blood for any angels or any other created beings because we are not created beings like unto the angels. Human beings were made in the image of God and after His likeness. Yet, many people refuse to acknowledge God as the Creator and that He is the Father of all mankind; whether you are good or bad, the Lord God is your heavenly Father. Thank God and give glory unto His name. Even in this wicked and sinful world, many do honor the Father and the Son, but there is a multitude that refuses to accept God.

Revelation 7:9-12 (KJV)
[9] After this I beheld, and, lo, a great multitude, which no man could number, of all nations, and kindreds, and people, and tongues, stood

before the throne, and before the Lamb, clothed with white robes, and palms in their hands;

¹⁰ And cried with a loud voice, saying, Salvation to our God which sitteth upon the throne, and unto the Lamb.

¹¹ And all the angels stood round about the throne, and *about* the elders and the four beasts, and fell before the throne on their faces, and worshipped God,

¹² Saying, Amen: Blessing, and glory, and wisdom, and thanksgiving, and honour, and power, and might, *be* unto our God for ever and ever. Amen.

God created the world "Universe" **Genesis 1:1 (KJV)** In the beginning God created the heaven and the earth.

God is the one and the only one that created the heavens and the earth, and not mankind. Mankind has absolutely nothing to do with the creation of anything concerning the heavens and the earth and all that is in them. Yes, we do make things from the created things that belong to God; however, God is the one who created all things.

Jesus Christ is the Son of God. He is not just the Son of God, He is the only begotten Son of the living God. There are no other people, angels, or things, whether seen or unseen, that was begotten of God; there is absolutely nothing else except Jesus Christ. Jesus Christ is the only one that is the begotten Son of God.

Jesus came forth from the Father, and the Father is in heaven; therefore, this proves that Jesus was in heaven first before He was manifested in the flesh here on earth. Everything that God does is always done in the spirit realm first, and then at the appointed time that He has put in place, we experience the manifestation of His plan in the natural or physical realm. How do we know this that Jesus was with the Father in the beginning? Many references direct us to the truth in the Bible scriptures.

John 1:1-4 (KJV)

[1] In the beginning was the Word, and the Word was with God, and the Word was God.

[2] The same was in the beginning with God.

[3] All things were made by him; and without him was not anything made that was made.

[4] In him was life; and the life was the light of men.

The first verse said, "In the beginning was the Word," and the **Word** means Jesus; this is telling us that Jesus was with the Father from the beginning - "the dateless past." As we continue to read the scriptures, we will find many other references that clearly inform us that Jesus is not only the begotten Son of God, but He is also God. Jesus Christ is not the Father, He is the Son, yet it pleases the Father to make the Son even Lord.

Colossians 1:12-17 (KJV)

[12] Giving thanks unto the Father, which hath made us meet to be partakers of the inheritance of the saints in light:

[13] Who hath delivered us from the power of darkness, and hath translated *us* into the kingdom of his dear Son:

[14] In whom we have redemption through his blood, *even* the forgiveness of sins:

[15] Who is the image of the invisible God, the firstborn of every creature:

[16] For by him were all things created, that are in heaven, and that are in earth, visible and invisible, whether *they be* thrones, or dominions, or principalities, or powers: all things were created by him, and for him:

[17] And he is before all things, and by him all things consist.

John 8:57-58 (KJV)

[57] Then said the Jews unto him, Thou art not yet fifty years old, and hast thou seen Abraham?

[58] Jesus said unto them, Verily, verily, I say unto you, Before Abraham was, I am.

As we read the first chapter of **St. John** and now the first chapter of **Colossians**, we should now have a clearer understanding of agreement in the knowledge of God's Son, Christ Jesus, that His deity is accurate, and accuracy is exact. As stated before, you will find other scriptures that prove the Deity of Jesus.

We have heard of Abraham, the father of faith unto righteousness. Jesus is telling those that still refuse to believe that He was with His Father from the beginning. Jesus is declaring unto us that before Abraham was, He already was. Jesus Christ is the I am, and He is the Alpha and Omega. The only person that would ever be born of a woman that can rightfully make this profound claim is Jesus. He is the only one, and not any other mankind, who is *I am the Alpha and the Omega,* **beginning and the end.** Jesus also declares that He is the *Alpha and the Omega,* the *first and the last.* It is written and cannot be altered; no matter how many people refuse to accept Jesus Christ in this earth, none of us can changes what God has spoken about His Son.

Jesus Christ came forth from the Father, and even now, Jesus is in heaven with the Father, as the scripture said, making intercession on our behalf to our God and heavenly Father.

Jesus is the Christ, meaning the anointed One. Therefore, we must agree that Christ Jesus, the anointed One, came to save all humanity from their sins. It does not make a difference what denomination or who your pastor is; they are not your God and Savior. Yes, there is only one GOD; however, it pleases the Father to put all things in the hands of His Son, Jesus.

Jesus Christ was before all things, whether seen or unseen, "visible or invisible." Jesus is the only one that God has sent into this wicked and sinful world to save all humanity from their sins. God made Jesus His Son to be Lord over humanity, and gave Him Authority over His Kingdom; it is written and cannot be changed, and will never change.

Jesus is the Son of God, and He came from the Father. Jesus is the image of the invisible God. Jesus Christ and the Father are one, and they are not personalities, but instead, they are one in oneness in all agreements.

Jesus came from heaven and took on human form to be like us, born of a virgin woman named Mary to die for the sins of all humanity, and by doing so, He died once for humanity to live again forever. Jesus left for us an example when He died that we too will also die, but there is hope for humanity. He rose from the dead victoriously, so also, we will rise from the dead in the resurrection in righteousness to be with Him forever. However, not all will rise from the dead in righteousness. All those who refuse to accept the Son of God as their Savior and live their life according to the word of God in righteousness will not have eternal life with the Lord Jesus Christ. They will live forever, but not with Jesus. They will spend their time with Satan, who is called the devil in hell. Is that what you want for your next life? Repent and worship the Lord and live.

John 5:28-29 (KJV)
28 Marvel not at this: for the hour is coming, in the which all that are in the graves shall hear his voice,
29 And shall come forth; they that have done good, unto the resurrection of life; and they that have done evil, unto the resurrection of damnation.

To be with Jesus Christ forever and never have to die again, we must accept Him as our Savior, meaning to be born again, and this means to be saved from our sins. The born again experience can only happen by the Spirit of God, and without this new birth, none shall inherit the Kingdom of God the Father. Jesus is the Savior of All humanity. If you are reading this book and haven't given your life to the only Savior of the world yet, please do not put it off. Make your decision now by asking the LORD God to forgive you of your sins, and let God know that you need Jesus, His Son, to come into your heart and live. ***Repent of your sins before it is too late!***

The Divine Will of God is to restore humanity and the earth to their original perfect state and function. The only way that God has chosen to do this is through His Son, Jesus. Jesus is the only one who the Father sent into this world to bring salvation to us. No human being can forgive another so that they can make it into heaven; only the Father and the Son can forgive human beings for their sins. Yes, we can forgive others for the wrong that they have done to us so that we will be in the right relationship with God and His Son, Jesus Christ, but we cannot save anyone.

The baby Jesus that many of us have celebrated His birthday in December and called the day Christmas is no longer a baby lying in a manger, and this we must teach to our children. This mighty Jesus of Nazareth is now a victorious Lord of lords, and He conquered Satan on the cross. He has grown up to be a man, and this Jesus defeated the devil for all mankind so that we can come back to God, our heavenly Father. Will you come back to God today? If yes, Jesus is waiting to wash and cleanse you so that He can present you to God, your heavenly Father in holiness!

The unity of God the Father, Jesus Christ the Son, and the Holy Ghost "Holy Spirit" are not three personalities, but rather, there is one God in three persons, and the three agree in oneness.

1 John 5:7 (KJV)

[7] For there are three that bear record in heaven, the Father, the Word, and the Holy Ghost: and these three are one.

GOD the Father is not one person divided into three personalities; there is one God, one begotten Son "Jesus," and one Holy Ghost. There are many references in the scriptures that give us this knowledge of Jesus Christ, but many of us are still unlearn about the truth of the God-Head.

Genesis 1:26 (KJV)

²⁶ And God said, Let us make man in our image, after our likeness: and let them have dominion over the fish of the sea, and over the fowl of the air, and over the cattle, and over all the earth, and over every creeping thing that creepeth upon the earth.

John 17:1 (KJV)

¹ These words spake Jesus, and lifted up his eyes to heaven, and said, Father, the hour is come; glorify thy Son, that thy Son also may glorify thee:

John 17:5 (KJV)

⁵ And now, O Father, glorify thou me with thine own self with the glory which I had with thee before the world was.

The scripture above clearly opens our eyes to knowledge for understanding to show us that Jesus Christ was having a conversation with His Father, who is in heaven while He was here on earth. Therefore, we must listen to the Lord God as He speaks to us by His Word, and stop letting people turn you into foolishness. Read and study the word of God for yourself and ask the Lord for the understanding of His written word by the Holy Spirit.

Three persons agree in heaven, God, who is the Father of the Lord Jesus and all humanity. Jesus Christ is the Son of God, and the Savior of all humankind. The Holy Ghost, is the Holy Spirit, and He is the Spirit of God, our Father, He the Holy Spirit is carrying out the work of the Father and the Son on this earth. Please let this settle in your spirit and mind and let us move on in the things of God with the understanding of who the Father, the Son, and the Holy Spirit truly is. Emmanuel, meaning God with us. GOD came to us in the form of man to save us from our sins, and He who came to us in the form of a man, His name is Jesus.

Matthew 1:23 (KJV)

23 Behold, a virgin shall be with child, and shall bring forth a son, and they shall call his name Emmanuel, which being interpreted is, God with us.

Jesus' name means **one who saves.** Christ means the **Anointing One.** In order to save the human race, God came to mankind in the form of a man to save us from our sins; God has been patient with humanity from the fall of man in the Garden of Eden, and it is still His will to restore humankind so that we can have a right relationship with Him just as Adam and Eve once had with God when they were in the Garden. Since humanity sinned against the LORD God, He came to us in the form of a man to pay the sin price. Man sinned; therefore, it would take a man to save sinful humanity, and there was no one among the human race that was found worthy of being the sacrificial Lamb without blemish.

Jesus is the only one that is the Son of man, and at the same time, he is the begotten Son of God. Jesus Christ is the only One God sees no blemishes in and find no sin in, other than Adam and Eve until they sinned. Jesus was the only man that ever walked this earth and was pure in all sense of purity. He was the only one that was suitable to die for the sins of all humanity.

This plan pleases the Father, the Son, and the Holy Ghost, "Holy Spirit." The Father, Jesus the Son, and the Holy Spirit are working on our behalf against the power of darkness so that we can live a life of victory on earth. Many believe in Jesus but give Him no reverence; many of us have disrespected Him daily. This Jesus, who many of us don't want to have anything to do with, you will see Him sitting on His throne, judging you and all sinners who have rejected Him while you were alive on the earth. Don't think that when you die in your sins that the living can pray for the dead "which is you" for your sins that you have committed against God and make it into heaven; it cannot happen, and it will never happen; God is not a God of slackness. The life that we live here on earth will determine which way we go when we all die.

Some people in the world are always fighting against each other for power. If someone merits a promotion on their job, someone, somewhere will seem to be jealous and envious, criticizing that person for the new status that they have gotten for his or her hard work. That is the sinful nature that Jesus came to deliver us from before we ended up in hell. Also, at times, depending on your career that you have chosen, some people will go back from birth to bring up your past life and remind you of them just because of jealousy. Please remember this, as we dig up and expose others among us, if your dirty life were known, you would be very ashamed, so why do it to other's. Be very careful of the hole that you are digging because one day, not long from now, the pit of your past will be exposed. Not many people are happy for each other's growth on this earth; there is always strife and hate towards one another. God sent Jesus to save us from all of these and many more hateful behaviors toward each other, but we don't want to listen. It is full time we obey God because hell is real, and the judgment to come shall come.

Lucifer, who is Satan, who is also called the "devil" before his rebellion in heaven, was one of God's archangels before he exalted himself above God in his heart. We come to know what happened to him after his rebellion. He was thrown out of heaven and one-third of angels followed him. Satan is our enemy, therefore, be careful of him. God is not our enemy, neither is Jesus, they are our friends. God loves us so much that He was willing to allow His only begotten Son to come and suffer for us, and then die for the human race. God gave His Son, Jesus to us, but many do not want anything to do with Him. Do you accept Jesus as your personal Savior as yet? If not, you need to do so right now before it is too late, because after death, no one that is alive can ask the Lord to forgiveness you of your sins, neither can you, because you are no more alive.

Repentance prayer: It is not hard to repent of your sins to the Lord; just speak these words and believe them in your heart.

Father God, I come to you in Jesus name, I acknowledge that I am a sinner, and I need my sins to be forgiven. I believe that Jesus Christ is your only begotten Son, who came and died for my sins and that He shed His blood on Calvary for the remission (forgiveness) of my sins. Therefore, Father God, it is my desire for Jesus Christ to be my Lord and Savior, so I ask of You, wash me and cleanse me with the blood of your Son, Jesus, in Jesus' name, Amen.

After you have given your life to Jesus as your Lord and Savior, you need to get a Bible if you haven't already got one and read it daily. The Bible is your instruction book (Guide Book) here on earth. You need to find a church that preaches the Bible, meaning the gospel of the Lord Jesus. Some may try to discourage you from the best decision that you will ever make in your entire life, but don't listen to them; some are instruments of Satan.

Get to know this man called Jesus very well because He is our only hope to be with God the Father. Jesus Christ is not just the Son of man, but rather, Jesus Christ is the only begotten Son of God, the Father, and He, Jesus, is Lord. Jesus was begotten of God the Father, meaning Jesus came forth from the Father, and the Holy Spirit carried out this Divine plan of God so that Jesus became a babe in the womb of a virgin woman named Mary.

Thank God that there was a young woman in this earth that God highly favored, and God used her as a vessel of honor to carry the man child, Jesus, in her womb. Did you know that even Mary, the mother of Jesus Christ, the anointed One, also needs Jesus, her Son, to save her from the sin nature? Many of you may disbelieve me right here, but this is not for contention at all if you know the scriptures; all human beings are sinners until they accept Jesus Christ as their Savior. Every human beings born of a woman need Jesus Christ precious blood upon them so that they can be wash and cleanse from unrighteousness, so that the Father can accept us.

Just because she gives birth to the Savoir does not mean she was sinless. She also needs her sins to be forgiven, and so does all other human beings, because all human beings are born in sin, and this is called the sin nature. Therefore, Mary cannot intercede for anyone's sins, only the sinless Jesus Christ, the Son of God, who is our High Priest in heaven. Please don't get offended by this statement based on your fundamental belief, as this is to bring millions upon millions of people closer to Jesus Christ of Nazareth instead of believing that man can intercede for man's sins. Have you forgotten already that the scripture said all mankind is born in sin? Remember that is why Jesus came to reconcile us to God by purchasing us from unrighteousness with His precious blood and death, and by doing so, He brings light into our hearts, which was once full of darkness. Jesus is the only One who can redeem us and present us to the Father; this is God's doing, and it is wonderful and glorious. ***Amen***

Remember this and do not forget it, please! Jesus Christ is the only one who can save humanity from their sins. No one or nothing else can do so, and if someone tells you otherwise, they are lying to you, and if you follow their advice, you are heading to the gate of hell, and hell will swallow you up. It is plain and simple as that, and it is the truth. If this is too bold or forward, please forgive my rudeness, but not for the truth. Remember this, hellfire is hotter than those words. Please listen to the Lord God speaking to us in His word, listen very carefully as He speaks to you when you read it. There is no other way to God the Father except through Jesus Christ, the Son, who is the Lord and Savior of all humanity.

John 14:6 (KJV)

⁶ Jesus saith unto him, I am the way, the truth, and the life: no man cometh unto the Father, but by me.

God, having foreknowledge of the fall of man in the Garden of Eden, has set in motion the plan to restore mankind to the original state of God and man before the deceit. Humanity needs to be saved from the terrible wrath that is to come from God at His appointed time. And because of that which will come upon all humankind, Jesus Christ was willing in obedience to the Father; He came to shed His blood and to die to redeem us from the wrath of Almighty God.

Therefore, we must be thankful to God for Christ Jesus for all that He has done for us on the cross at Calvary. Jesus brings salvation to all of us and we have to accept Him or else we will not get it.

Hear the word of the LORD God and Jesus before it is too late, repent of your sins all ye nations of the earth, and turn from your wicked ways unto God in the only name that is given under heaven, which mankind might be saved, and that name is Jesus.

It is all about Christ Jesus: The anointed One who came to save all mankind from their sins.

Many people have already died in their sins and are now in hell waiting to be judged for the things that they have done while they were alive. They died in their sins because they disobey God and His Son. They refuse to love God according to the scriptures, and they also refuse to love their neighbors as they love themselves.

Again, only Jesus Christ of Nazareth can save human beings from their sin. Anyone who claims to be the Christ is a liar; they are not and will never be one. Anyone who claims that Jesus Christ is not the only way that mankind can be saved is also a liar. All ye nations who have an ear to hear, hear ye the Spirit of God, and do not let mankind like yourself give you false hope and promises. Listen to the Spirit of God. Only the Son of God can save people from their sins—absolutely Him alone.

Many have put their trust in mankind and turned their back on the only One that can save them from the wrath to come. Listen carefully: I am asking you to get the word of God, the Holy Bible, and read it for yourself and depend upon the Holy Spirit to reveal the mystery in the written word. If you and your loved ones died in the state of sin, there is no returning from the dead to make things right with God. That's it, your faith is what you believe in and live for at the time of death; in that state, you remain eternally. If you died in unrighteousness, you are sealed in sin, and if you died in righteousness, you are sealed in righteousness.

There are no resting places or holding places for anyone that died in sin to work out their righteousness. Anyone that is teaching this doctrine is deceiving you. This is it, right here on earth; this is where we live for God in righteousness and holiness to go to heaven. And all those who choose to live in unrighteousness in this earth will find themselves in hell. This is not a place for any human being; it is not a good place; neither is it a pleasant place where anyone in their right senses would want to go. No matter how wicked anyone is in their heart, if they only have a mindset to turn away from their wickedness and repent of their sins, Jesus will forgive them, and that person will receive eternal life from the Lord Jesus and live forever. How about you? Do you want to live forever and never have to die the second death in the lake of fire?

We teach and preach about how hell is a terrible place to end up for the rest of someone's life and forget about the lake of fire. You are encouraged to read the Prophecy of Jesus Christ in the book of Revelation. We believe that everyone that dies in their sin is going to hell regardless of who they are, because of their wicked heart and sinful life that they live while they were alive. Please reconsider your knowledge or get knowledge of God's holy word.

Revelation 20:10 (KJV)
[10] And the devil that deceived them was cast into the lake of fire and brimstone, where the beast and the false prophet *are*, and shall be tormented day and night for ever and ever.

Revelation 20:14-15 (KJV)

[14] And death and hell were cast into the lake of fire. This is the second death.

[15] And whosoever was not found written in the book of life was cast into the lake of fire.

It is what it is! You die in unrighteousness; you go to hell. You die in righteousness; you go straight to heaven to be with the Lord. No more pain, no more hunger, no more earthly agony from humanity in whichever way. No more sorrows, no more suffering, and no more tears. All Christians will be in the presence of the Lord in heaven, where everything is perfect for the time that is mentioned in the scripture, and after that, we will follow Jesus as he returns to the earth to rule with Him. The enemy has enticed so many of us to pursue the things of this world in unrighteousness, and by doing so, we have taken our eyes off the Savior. The enemy is smart; he knows exactly the things that he can get you to focus on, the things that the mind and the flesh enjoy.

Jesus wants the children of God to focus on spiritual things. The spirit, soul, and body are to line up with the Holy Spirit and the word of God so that we all can enjoy the things of God here on earth before going home to meet Him. There is nothing in this entire world worth dying for, absolutely nothing, then why are wicked people killing each other for things that none of them can take to hell or heaven? Many of us, in our foolish ways, were caught up with all of this madness to get more and more, forgetting what is essential, and died a sinner, then loses their soul and life for eternity to join Satan in hell.

Mark 8:36-38 (KJV)

[36] For what shall it profit a man, if he shall gain the whole world, and lose his own soul?

[37] Or what shall a man give in exchange for his soul?

[38] Whosoever therefore shall be ashamed of me and of my words in this adulterous and sinful generation; of him also shall the Son of man be ashamed, when he cometh in the glory of his Father with the holy angels.

People and nations of the earth, the only rewarding life that any one of us can live, with rewards that are beyond our comprehension, is to live a life pleasing and acceptable unto the LORD God. Being a Christian does not mean that your life will be boring, as many may think; on the contrary, Jesus Christ gives God's children peace that passes all understanding and joy that we never knew before, and Jesus even gives us heaven too. What more do you need why you are killing yourself and others just to have plenty and after your death someone gets it?

John 10:10 (KJV)
[10] The thief cometh not, but for to steal, and to kill, and to destroy: I am come that they might have life and that they might have *it* more abundantly.

As we live our lives in this world as a sinner, there are rules that we must follow, and these rules are laws, policies, procedures, instructions, and more. When we do not adhere to those regulations, there are consequences. Well, it is the same and even more with the things of God. The standard of God is not like the standard of humanity. Humanity lies to get out of their problems. We compromise to have our way, and when we cannot have things our way, we fight and argue with our mouth, spewing out poison and death from the heart and believe that everything is okay with our behavior. But far from it, this behavior is of Satan. Those behaviors are disrespectful, and favors are called compromise or double standard for the advantage of some above others.

Sometimes it seems as if there are different laws for different people in this world. Those that are rich and are known seem to get better treatment in receiving favor from man, but the poor and middle class sometimes are treated indifferently just because their status is not like some others. The Lord does not want anyone of us to favor one above the other person; we must treat one another the same. Can you imagine if Jesus were prejudice or favor only some of us, there would be no hope for humanity, absolutely none? Jesus, when He went to the cross, went for all, and not for some. With the Lord, Jesus does not compromise His words to please society, He is not seeking friends. When He speaks, the Lord expects us to follow His command, and failure to do so is sin, and sin is death. We must be thankful to the Lord God that He loves all of us the same, even though some of us are good, and many may be harmful. However, when it comes to God's standard of excellence, there is no double standard. If you are right, you are just right, and if you are wrong, you are just wrong, and this is the "absolute truth."

Your yes should be yes, and your nay should be nay. God deals with absolute truth, and this is the way the Lord wants all of His children to live. Do we want to have the mind of Christ? Well then, Christians, we must start living a life of truth and not of lies.

Philippians 2:5 (KJV)
5 Let this mind be in you, which was also in Christ Jesus:

Only Jesus can help us to live a sincere and pure life to please our God. People make promises, and they are not sure if they can keep it, because situation or conditions can arise that causes them not to keep their promises. But for all the promises that God promised His children, He will never go back on His words. So, who should we wholly put our trust in? Only in the Lord Jesus!

Let us, therefore, children of the living God, and through the saving grace in Jesus Christ, obey the word of God that was given to us to live by while living on this earth. We are all children of the Creator, the only One who loves us despite our wrong. But that does not mean that He puts up with our slackness. God does not know how to hate humanity because there is no unrighteousness in Him, like us, who sometimes hate each other. God is love, and He does not hate anyone; he only knows how to love because He is love.

1 John 4:8 (KJV)
8 He that loveth not knoweth not God; for God is love.

CHAPTER THREE

Who is this man, Jesus?

Why are so many people in love with this man Jesus Christ, even though they haven't met Him face to face yet? Who can this man be that even the created beings in heaven will bow at His feet? Who is this man? Why are so many people getting killed just because they love Him, and many are still being kill because of this one man? Why are so many people feeling threatened by Him?

Philippians 2:10-11 (KJV)
[10] That at the name of Jesus every knee should bow, of *things* in heaven, and *things* in earth, and *things* under the earth;
[11] And *that* every tongue should confess that Jesus Christ *is* Lord, to the glory of God the Father.

So many people have been killed just because they love this man Jesus. But why? He is not here in person, so He does not threaten anyone. Many are in prison just because they dearly love this man Jesus. Does anybody know who He is? It is said that this man died so that all humanity who accepted Him will have eternal life and reign with Him forever.

It is also said that this man, Jesus, shed His blood on the cross at Calvary for the remission of mankind's sins. It gets even more enjoyable. He gave up His life, and He died, and He was buried, and in three days,

He rose from the grave victoriously. Now this man, Jesus, is with His Father and our Father in heaven, making intercessions on our behalf. This man, Jesus, the Son of the living God, is in heaven waiting for the time that is set forth by the Father alone when He shall come from heaven to carry the children of God out of this wicked and sinful world. These children are those who died in righteousness and all those who are presently living in righteousness. Will you be one of them?

O yes, glory hallelujah to our Lord and King. He once walked this earth, and He is presently in heaven at the right hand of God. But not long from now, which no man knows except the Father, Jesus Christ will be coming back again to receive us unto Himself. We better be ready, because if we are not, many will be left behind, and it will not be a pleasant time in those days. Read the word of God for yourself and come to know the truth.

1 Thessalonians 4:16-17 (KJV)

16 For the Lord himself shall descend from heaven with a shout, with the voice of the archangel, and with the trump of God: and the dead in Christ shall rise first:

17 Then we which are alive *and* remain shall be caught up together with them in the clouds, to meet the Lord in the air: and so shall we ever be with the Lord.

Somebody, please tell me, who is this man Jesus? This man has done so many wonderful things for every one of us. Many people do not recognize it because they believe it is all about their hard work, their educated abilities. Yes, I am not saying that our hard work does not contribute to our achievements. However, what could we have done or achieved in this earth if it was not for Jesus, the only begotten Son of the LORD God? Yes, the LORD God blesses us through His Son, because of what Jesus has done for us on the cross. We have the word of God, and all we have to do is read it for ourselves and the LORD God and His Son, Jesus, will speak to us through the written word, and the

Holy Spirit will be the One who will give us the interpretations and the understanding of the written words. Humanity does not deserve such love and kindness from the Father, but because of grace and mercy by Jesus Christ, the mercy of God is extended toward us. The LORD God is not man, and What He says that He will do, consider it done.

Numbers 23:19 (KJV)

[19] God *is* not a man, that he should lie; neither the son of man, that he should repent: hath he said, and shall he not do *it*? or hath he spoken, and shall he not make it good?

He just keeps on loving us regardless of our disobedient ways. Read the word of God for yourself that is in The Holy Bible. Read about the love that the Father has for all humanity. In this book, the Bible details the love that the only begotten Son of the Father has for the children of the living God. He loves us regardless of who we are or where we come from; however, that does not mean He agrees with our ungodly behavior.

Nations of the earth, hurry up before it is too late for you. The LORD God is a Holy and Just God, and He does not put up with human folly. If it were not for the blood of Jesus Christ that was shed on the cross at Calvary, we probably would not be here today. Nevertheless, we are here, and for this reason and many more, we owe Him our life, and we should praise Him. Read the Old Testament scriptures, and you will find out that the penalty for sin is death. Most of the time, after the Almighty warned them over and over and they refused to obey, many of them died in their sin because of ignorance, by failing to obey the commandment of God.

The LORD God warned the people of the Old Testament over and over to turn from their wicked ways and repent for their errors, but many refused and they died in their sins. The Lord is still warning us to turn, and we are not following God's command. When they refuse to follow God's instruction, the Father, who does not tolerate sin, consumed many in the wilderness. Let us all learn from the past experiences of those before us; we do not have to experience the wrath of the living God. If we only accept God's only begotten Son, JESUS CHRIST, and confess our sins to God in Jesus' name, He is faithful and just to forgive us of our sins.

1 John 1:8-10 (KJV)

[8] If we say that we have no sin, we deceive ourselves, and the truth is not in us.

[9] If we confess our sins, he is faithful and just to forgive us *our* sins, and to cleanse us from all unrighteousness.

[10] If we say that we have not sinned, we make him a liar, and his word is not in us.

Who is this man Jesus that death could not hold Him in the grave? He is greater than death. It is written that He went to hell and took the keys of death and the grave. Therefore, when a Christian "Child of God" dies, death cannot hold them too because immediately at death, the spirit and soul leave their body to be with the Lord.

2 Corinthians 5:8 (KJV)

[8] We are confident, *I say*, and willing rather to be absent from the body, and to be present with the Lord.

This man, Jesus, came forth from the LORD God the Father, whose dwelling place is in heaven, and this place called heaven is far beyond human comprehension. Heaven is not a place that any human being can take a flight to. Only God, the Father, and the Lord Jesus Christ can allow anyone to enter heaven, by the Spirit of God who prepared us for the journey, whether in the body or the spirit. Only those who have their spiritual body can go; however, except for two persons whom the scripture told us of, who have not yet experienced death. Enoch and Elijah are in heaven with their natural body. The Lord God is so holy that everything around Him is sacred. The LORD God is an Awesome God, He is a Mighty God, and He is Sovereign. He commands, and things come into existence. He calls forth, and things appear for His excellent pleasure. Heaven is the place God lives, and Jesus Christ is God's only begotten Son. The first man, Adam, was made after the image and likeness of the Trinity, but Jesus was not made like unto Adam, but rather, Jesus was begotten of the Father.

Genesis 1:26-27 (KJV)

[26] And God said, Let us make man in our image, after our likeness: and let them have dominion over the fish of the sea, and over the fowl of the air, and over the cattle, and over all the earth, and over every creeping thing that creepeth upon the earth.
[27] So God created man in his *own* image, in the image of God created he him; male and female created he them.

Many people in this world do not accept Jesus as the Son of God. Is it because He is a man like us human being? We must accept Jesus Christ as our Lord and Savior. Because of this man, Christ Jesus, we are still alive today. If we were under the law of GOD, some of us, if not most of us, would be consumed because of the life that we are now living, and breaking the law is death. The question may be asked, what is that life? Look carefully around you and you will see all manner of **ungodly** or **unrighteous** lifestyles that are against the will of God for our lives.

Please tell me more about this man named Jesus. He is so wonderful, kind, loving, and He is precious. He is the only One that can save humanity from their sins, and there will never be any human being that has the power and the authority to do so. Humanity can never give eternal life to another, but Jesus can. If Jesus is the only One who is the doorway to heaven to be with the Father, I am ready to give this man Christ Jesus a try because my life is not getting any better living in sin.

I want to give myself away entirely to the Lord of all lords and the King of all kings, and His name is Jesus. Jesus, please take my heart, my soul, life, and body, and all that I am. I give them all to you, Lord Jesus; I desire to live for God. Lord Jesus, even now, please come into my heart and live… cleanse me, oh Lord, from all unrighteousness.

Who is this man Jesus that the wind obeyed Him? The boisterous waves calm at His command. He even walks on water. He did not want to swim, but rather, He chose to walk on water and that He did! And Jesus also gave one of His disciples the authority to walk on water, which he did. He fed many with not enough food; the Father honors His Son, Jesus, and multiplied the loaf and fishes.

He cast evil spirits out of people, causing them to be freed from the oppression and bondage of the enemy, "the devil." Jesus came to set the captives free from Satan prison that many of us were in, and even now, many are still in prison, and only Jesus can set them free. The bondage of prison by their sin allows the devil to steal their mind. The devil will kill them and then destroy their lives just because they are refusing the only One who can free them from Satan oppressions, and oppression leads to depressions.

Many have accepted the call to repentance for their lives. Still, there are so many more that are not taking the invitation of salvation seriously for their lives, believing that they have time, or maybe they do not believe in this salvation plan that God's Son brings for us humanity.

2 Timothy 2:26 (KJV)
[26] And *that* they may recover themselves out of the snare of the devil, who are taken captive by him at his will.

Hurry up, unbelievers, before it is too late to give your life unto the Lord Jesus Christ. He is the only One who can save you from your sins. Christians, do not for one moment live your Christian life as you once did before you gave your life to Jesus Christ. You are now children of the living God, and He expects all of His children to live a holy life.

Who is this man called Jesus? The scripture said that Jesus is over all principalities.

Ephesians 1:21-22 (KJV)
[21] Far above all principality, and power, and might, and dominion, and every name that is named, not only in this world, but also in that which is to come:
[22] And hath put all *things* under his feet, and gave him *to be* the head over all *things* to the church,

Colossians 2:10 (KJV)
[10] And ye are complete in him, which is the head of all principality and power:

Jesus is, above all principalities and power. Principalities do have more power than humanity, yet this man, Jesus, who is the Son of man, has God exalted above all powers and put all things under His feet. Jesus is not just a mere man, He is Lord, and the sooner some of us come to our senses and accept who Jesus is, the better our lives will be. Yes, the powers of darkness are indeed more powerful than any humanity in the natural, but we are more than conquerors in the spirit. What does the Bible say?

1 John 4:4 (KJV)
[4] Ye are of God, little children, and have overcome them: because greater is he that is in you, than he that is in the world.

Zechariah 4:6 (KJV)
[6] Then he answered and spake unto me, saying, This *is* the word of the LORD unto Zerubbabel, saying, Not by might, nor by power, but by my spirit, saith the LORD of hosts.

Yes, the enemy will come against the children of God to discourage them from their faith in God, but we must not give up or give in to his devices. It is his job to fight against us. However, we too must fight against him in holiness. Children of God, do not let anyone discourage you from following Jesus. If you should listen to them, whoever it may be, can they save you from your sins? Can they give you eternal life? Can they wash and cleanse you with the blood of Jesus?

Who is this man who takes water and turns it into wine? His name is Jesus. Something to think about: Why would the mother of Jesus, Mary, want her Son to turn water into wine? I believe that the mother of Jesus, Mary, has seen her Son in action before that, and she has come to know precisely what her Son was able to do. Jesus Christ was not just her Son, but He is the Son of God, and Jehovah God is a miracle-working God. We now know that Jesus is like His Father; He is a miracle-working Savior.

The Bible said this about Jesus,

Isaiah 9:5-7 (KJV)
6 For unto us a child is born, unto us a son is given: and the government shall be upon his shoulder: and his name shall be called Wonderful, Counsellor, The mighty God, The everlasting Father, The Prince of Peace. 7 Of the increase of *his* government and peace *there shall be* no end, upon the throne of David, and upon his kingdom, to order it, and to establish it with judgment and with justice from henceforth even forever. The zeal of the LORD of hosts will perform this.

This man Jesus is not just a man; He is more than just a man. He is Jesus, meaning one who saves. He is Emmanuel, meaning God with us. Therefore, when Jesus was here on earth, He was God with humanity manifested in the flesh.

Jesus is Wonderful. He is the most precious person among all mankind that would ever be born of a woman. Jesus Christ is a Counselor to our soul. Whatever it is that we need counseling in, Jesus is our Counselor. Even though He allows other counselors to counsel us in godliness, some do not follow the Counselor of all counselors.

Jesus is the mighty God. Oh yes, do you not remember that Jesus is Lord, and that is why He is the mighty God, and all mankind must honor and praise Him? But we know that it is not so because of the wickedness in many. Jesus Christ is The everlasting Father to all humanity. Oh yes, this is what the scriptures say. Jesus is The Prince of Peace; no one can give us peace like Jesus. He will give us peace that passeth all understanding. When a person has the peace of God that passeth all knowledge, even during turmoil, they will be comforted because Peace is in them. Jesus is Lord, and we must lift His name above every name in this earth that God may glorify Jesus, His Son in this earth, to the glory of God the Father.

Brothers, sisters, and unbelievers, Jesus Christ is the only begotten Son of God. He is the only One who can save us from our sins through His death and the shedding of His blood at Calvary. In those acts alone, provisions were made for our salvation. Please do not listen to the lies that many are spreading that Jesus is not the only way. Who do you believe, God or man? Believe the words of God. Jesus Christ is the One and the only One that can save you and bring you into the presence of the Almighty God. ***Amen***

CHAPTER FOUR

This man, Jesus, is the only One that can save humanity

This man, Jesus, is the only One that can save us from our sins, and the reason for this is:

Acts 4:10-12 (KJV)
[10] Be it known unto you all, and to all the people of Israel, that by the name of Jesus Christ of Nazareth, whom ye crucified, whom God raised from the dead, *even* by him doth this man stand here before you whole.
[11] This is the stone which was set at nought of you builders, which is become the head of the corner.
[12] Neither is there salvation in any other: for there is none other name under heaven given among men, whereby we must be saved.

Every person is born in sin— "sinful nature". Even though when we were babies, we did not know right or wrong, good or evil, until we get matured in our senses to know right and wrong. The sinful nature can be seen even in a little child if you know what the sinful nature is. We do not have to get mature. Just look at a baby. When you tell a baby not to touch, what do they do? Sometimes immediately, they do exactly what you told them not to do. This is the sin nature that is in all of us. However, babies do not have the senses to comprehend right and wrong.

The sinful nature in us is to disobey the will of GOD, and when we do so, that is when sin manifests itself in all manner of unrighteousness, and it does not matter who we are.

The wrong that we choose to do will always displease the LORD God; however, because of the LORD God who loves us so much before the World was, He made a way to save all mankind from their sins. Because He is the Sovereign One, having foreknowledge of our behavior, He has ordained our redemption through His Son, Jesus.

Because of what Adam and Eve did in the Garden of Eden, they should have died right there. However, because of the mercy of God, He did not destroy them. But instead, God has a plan to save the human race. The Lord Jesus Christ is the begotten Son of God our Father; "Jesus, one who saves" came to earth and gave His life for us so that God can reconcile us to Himself and so that we can be sons and daughters of the true and living GOD of righteousness.

From the beginning, with Adam and Eve, GOD and man, heaven and earth were one, but because both Adam and Eve allowed themselves to be deceived by the devil, the sin nature entered into humanity. This one-act through disobedience to God has caused the world to experience the manifestation of what sin is. People against God. Animals are eating each other. People are destroying each other lives. The earth is no longer stable, and the weather system is unstable, causing terrible storms, hurricanes, earthquakes, volcanoes eruption, and more. People are killing for money, and men are raping women and young girls. There are sicknesses and diseases; viruses, harmful bacteria, and germs; cheating and stealing, and so much more. These are not good, and all of those and more are not God's perfect will for humanity. Because of sin, all those things and all that is not of God is the manifestation of Satan, the devil, and Jesus Christ of Nazareth came from the Father to save us from them and the wrath of God to come. The works of the devil are death, but the work of God is life everlasting.

Jesus Christ is the only One that can save humanity from their sins. The propaganda, which is of the devil, that some people are spreading that there are other ways we can be saved and get to heaven, and that is a lie. Please do not believe them; there is one that is greater than them that is speaking, and He is the Holy Spirit. First, run for your spiritual life; second, run for your physical life, because everyone who believes these lies is heading for destruction, both here and now and after the natural or physical death experience.

Read the word of God for yourself so that you will know the truth about heaven and hell, and to know that Jesus Christ is the only way to God. Failure to obey the truth and believe lies from those who are teaching and preaching deceit, you will wake up in hell thinking that you were doing the right thing. No, you are not doing the right thing. If you believe that there are other ways to heaven other than Jesus Christ, the Son of the living God, then He did not need to come and go through all the suffering He went through. He did not need to shed His blood if there were another way for our sins to be forgiven. He did not have to die for us if there was another way to God the Father. If you believe those lies out there, you are also a part-taker of their lies. However, if you will read the word of God for yourself and go to the House of God where the pastors are not watering down the word of God, they will teach and preach the word of truth to you, under the power of the Holy Spirit of God.

Jesus Christ is the only One that GOD sent into this world to give His life to save humanity from their sins. Anyone who claims that they are Jesus and that they can forgive you of your sins and save you so that you will go to heaven are liars, so do not believe them. They, too, will go to hell according to the scriptures. We must know when we have been deceived. Anyone who proclaims that they are Jesus, please do not listen to him/her, because that person is preaching heresy.

Revelation 21:8 (KJV)

[8] But the fearful, and unbelieving, and the abominable, and murderers, and whoremongers, and sorcerers, and idolaters, and all liars, shall have their part in the lake which burneth with fire and brimstone: which is the second death.

Jesus is the only One that suffered the agony of pain for our sins. Jesus is the only One who shed His blood on the cross at Calvary for the remission of our sins. Jesus is the only One who died, was buried, and in three days, GOD raised His Son by the Holy Spirit from the grave victoriously. Jesus is the only One that is right now at the right hand of God in heaven.

Romans 8:11-12 (KJV)

But if the Spirit of him that raised up Jesus from the dead dwell in you, he that raised up Christ from the dead shall also quicken your mortal bodies by his Spirit that dwelleth in you.

No other man or woman will ever be worthy to die for another person's sin; therefore, let us move on and accept the Son of God, because He is the only way, and He is the truth and the life.

John 14:6 (KJV)

[6] Jesus saith unto him, I am the way, the truth, and the life: no man cometh unto the Father, but by me.

By the way, GOD, the Father, is the only Holy Father, and Jesus is the Lamb of God who gave His life for us. Many people in this world have a powerful effect upon others in this world, and some of them are convincing many to believe that Jesus is not the only way and that we do not need a blood wash cleansing purification for our sins. Oh, yes, we do need someone to die for us, and He already did, and His name is Jesus! Yes, we need someone to shed His blood for our sins, and His name is Jesus. Therefore, we owe the Lord our life because He gave His life for us.

Jesus came forth from the Father to be the perfect sacrifice for us unto God, the Father. Jesus Christ gave His life for us so that we will have life forever. However, this everlasting life does not come to you by not doing anything. For us to have this eternal life that is in Christ Jesus, we must confess our sins to the LORD God in the name of His Son, Jesus Christ, and we must also believe that Jesus Christ is the Son of God, and from that moment, you will begin to live your life according to the word of God.

Romans 10:9 (KJV)
9 That if thou shalt confess with thy mouth the Lord Jesus, and shalt believe in thine heart that God hath raised him from the dead, thou shalt be saved.

1 John 4:14-15 (KJV)
14 And we have seen and do testify that the Father sent the Son *to be* the Saviour of the world.
15 Whosoever shall confess that Jesus is the Son of God, God dwelleth in him, and he in God.

To all the nations, do not only rely on the words from the pastor's mouth because many false preachers come in the name of the Lord Jesus. Read the word for yourself, so that you will know if you are being taught, thus saith the Lord according to His holy word. However, some things are written in the Bible that is not easily understood; what you need to do is this, get a good study Bible that will help you, but most importantly, God does speak to His children too. He doesn't speak to His prophets alone; God also speaks to His children. What we need to do is to have a relationship with the Lord and seek God in prayer for an understanding of His word. He wants you to know Him so that you can live a holy life unto Him, and the Holy Spirit will help you.

By now, I pray that you have come to understand the truth about the Father and the Son, whose name is Jesus. No man or woman in this entire Universe could ever die and shed their blood for anyone to be saved. It cannot happen, and it will never happen! Everyone that is born of a woman, born with the sinful nature to sin, and because of that, all of us need a Savior, and that person is Jesus.

Jesus was not born with a sinful nature like us because His Father is not man; nevertheless, He faced all manner of temptation as we do, but He did not yield to any of them. Jesus did not come from man, but rather, Jesus came from God. The difference between Jesus and us is that he has one Father, and we have two fathers. Jesus' Father does not have a sinful nature, but our earthly father does. Nevertheless, He was still, like us, born of a woman.

Again, we have two fathers—first, we have our heavenly Father and then our earthly father. Why is God our first Father? Because He is the One who gave us to our father and mother before our parents ever met each other to marry and have children. Our heavenly Father already knew us because we were spirit and soul first, then our spirit and soul are joined with our earthly body.

When we sin against our first Father "GOD," we have done wrong, and we need to ask Him to forgive us, which He will do. When our heavenly Father forgives us, we are forgiven for the mistake that we have done, and God does not see that sin that He forgives us of again. By asking the Lord God to wash us with the blood of Jesus Christ, we are cleansed from unrighteousness. Because of the sin nature that is in us, we always need to ask God to forgive us because we sin in our minds, thoughts, and imagination; for example, looking down on people as if you are better than them. There are so many ways that we do sin against God, and Jesus can help.

A little more explanation. Many of us have sinned in simple things such as: thinking bad things about someone and desiring to sleep with another man or woman. Just thinking wickedness in our heart is sinful. Therefore, we always need to examine ourselves by judging our ways and thoughts. So, we always need to call on the name of the

Lord to wash us anew so that we can be clean, and this is where Jesus comes in. He is the only one that our first Father "GOD" has ordained and certified to die and shed His precious blood for the forgiveness of humanity.

The blood of Jesus is the only blood that is free from impurity; this is why His blood is so precious, the only blood that can purge us from our filthiness. And our heavenly Father can now look upon us as righteous children again. Why again? Because we were lost and now the blood of His Son, Jesus, washed us and made us clean again, giving us the right to have the relationship as Father, sons, and daughters to the true and living God.

It will not be easy to live the life of Christianity in this wicked and sinful world. Why? Because there are some people like you who are going around telling lies and trying to confuse many, especially those that do not already know the truth that Jesus Christ is the only way to your first Father, who is GOD. There are so many more things that are in the world that enticed many to go back into the world, and because they went back, they have lost their way. Also, some people hate Christians, but do not worry and we art not to worry anyway, because you know where you are going and where they will be if they do not turn from their wicked and sinful ways.

We have an enemy, he is the first enemy to all humanity, and that is Satan, also known as the devil. However, his original name was Lucifer. He does not love any human being; he hates us with passion and wants to destroy us and get us to be where he will be for eternity, and this place is called hell; however, the scripture tells us that death and hell will be cast into the lake of fire.

The devil is not what many believe he is; he was an archangel. **Ezekiel 28:11-28** tell us how beautiful he was created until he desired in his heart to be like GOD. So, he is not a man figure in a red suit, horns, and pitchfork. Believe the word of God: Satan and the demon spirit or "evil spirits" are powerful, and they are fighting against humanity to destroy us. Thank God for Jesus who defeated the devil on the cross so humanity now has hope in God. People of the earth, do not just live to live as if you are doing it all by yourself; it is because of Almighty God that we are alive on this earth.

It is not hard to understand; some people do not believe that there is a place called hell. Ok, if human beings are in hell because they have refused the gospel of Christ Jesus and rejected the Savior, this tells us that everyone, including Satan, will be cast into the lake of fire.

Revelation 20:9-10 (KJV)

⁹ And they went up on the breadth of the earth, and compassed the camp of the saints about, and the beloved city: and fire came down from God out of heaven, and devoured them.

¹⁰ And the devil that deceived them was cast into the lake of fire and brimstone, where the beast and the false prophet *are*, and shall be tormented day and night for ever and ever.

Hell is real. Therefore, to all those who are now saved by grace, do not allow anyone or things to cause you to return back into the world of darkness from which Christ has delivered you from. Do not lose your salvation in Christ Jesus. Remember that Jesus will never reject anyone; we are the ones who rejected the Son of God.

Sinners, you need to repent, meaning turn away from the wickedness and evil that you are doing in this world. Many of you are not wicked; you are good, and the Lord expected all of us to be good, but you are not saved. There is one thing that is missing, and that is to surrender your life to Jesus Christ and begin to live a righteous life according to the word of God. Many people are doing good works in this world, but these good deeds cannot save them, neither will it allow anyone to inherit the kingdom of heaven. It is not about the good works you are doing, but by confessing your sins to God and believing that Jesus Christ is the Son of God, putting your trust in Him and asking Him to come into your heart and live there, you will be saved. It is only Jesus that can save humanity from all their sins.

Sinners, you must come to Jesus and repent of your sins and mean it, and He will wash your sins away and sanctify your heart, mind, and soul, and the Holy Ghost will continue working on you, preparing you to be received by God through His Son, Jesus.

Do not let anyone tell you other than what the scriptures say. Jesus Christ is the one and only one, and He is the only way to the Father who is in heaven. The Lord Jesus loves you.

Amen

CHAPTER FIVE

God Gave Jesus His name

Everything about Jesus is divine. Even though Jesus was the Son of man while living on the earth, at the same time, He was the Son of God. Even though Jesus was man, He was also God, and God was with us, walking, talking, teaching, and correcting those that were there at the time. Even now, Jesus is still speaking to us through the written words of God, as He did back then by the ministering of the gospel under the anointing of the Holy Spirit.

Thank God for His Holy Spirit, who moved upon the prophets and Apostles to write the acts of the Father and His Son, leaving for us principles and examples that we must adhere to and the acceptance of Jesus Christ. Father God has shared the history of how this man child would be born on this earth and what His name should be called.

Matt: 1-21 (KJV)
20 But while he thought on these things, behold, the angel of the Lord appeared unto him in a dream, saying, Joseph, thou son of David, fear not to take unto thee Mary thy wife: for that which is conceived in her is of the Holy Ghost. 21And she shall bring forth a son, and thou shalt call his name JESUS: for he shall save his people from their sins.

Luke 1:31 (KJV)
And, behold, thou shalt conceive in thy womb, and bring forth a son, and shalt call his name JESUS

Matt 1:20-23 (KJV)
20 But while he thought on these things, behold, the angel of the Lord appeared unto him in a dream, saying, Joseph, thou son of David, fear not to take unto thee Mary thy wife: for that which is conceived in her is of the Holy Ghost. 21And she shall bring forth a son, and thou shalt call his name JESUS: for he shall save his people from their sins. 22Now all this was done, that it might be fulfilled which was spoken of the Lord by the prophet, saying, 23Behold, a virgin shall be with child, and shall bring forth a son, and they shall call his name Emmanuel, which being interpreted is, God with us.

We are loved by Him, and we love Him too

Jesus came to save people from their sins because everyone born of a woman is born with the sinful nature in them, and because of that, we all need someone who would die for us, giving His life for us. And it did happen, as that someone is Jesus. He came and died for humanity, and this is why all those who accepted Him loved Him so much.

Everything about Jesus is hated by Satan and all those who are very close to the devil. Satan and many of his followers hate Christians. Jesus has already warned us that we will be hated because of Him. The difference between Jesus and Satan is, the devil represents hate, but Jesus represents love. Say no to the devil and live. Jesus did not do anything wrong to us. We are the ones with the problems, always sinning against God and His Christ. Before we were born, Jesus loved us. Hear this: even though Satan exalts himself against the Lord in his heart and rebel against God, and he was sentenced to everlasting punishment, do you know that God still loves him? This is the same for those who refused the calling to repentance for their lives; God still loves you. All those who died in sin and are in hell at this moment, God still loves them.

Remember that humanity was made in the image and likeness of God the Father; therefore, He will always love us, His children, whether we are good or bad. Do not let someone tell you otherwise. If you are not a follower of Jesus at the moment, it doesn't mean that He does not love you. Yes, the Lord wants the very best for everyone, and He will not stop keeping the door open to get you to His Son, Jesus. However, we are the ones that need to take the bold steps to accept His Son, Jesus, so that we will not have to experience the punishment that awaits all those who were living on earth and die in sin.

Satan has been trying for humanity to disown Jesus Christ, and many have obeyed Satan. Those who are in authority have bought into the trick of the enemy "devil or Satan." Many businesses do not want their employees to say Merry Christmas; however, they do not mind the money that their business makes from people, whether saved or unsaved, during the Christmas season. Many are people-pleasers, afraid to lose money. Because of money, many business people are going to hell, as they are dealing with unjust judgment.

Even in the education system, the devil has infiltrated the learning institutions, teaching lies and disbeliefs. During graduation, those that choose to honor their heavenly Father and Jesus Christ, their Lord and Savior, cannot do it because their speeches are censored.

Without any investigation, if anyone of those students chooses to honor and praise their teachers, it would not be a problem, but the One who wakes them up in the morning cannot be spoken of at any time without some sort of problem. This act is of the devil. This is what he does: he promotes people and self but not Jesus. He tries to lift himself above God, but he was abased, and hell is his place of punishment in due time. He will then be cast into the lake of fire. Do you want to join him?

For many, it is okay to honor men, but it becomes a problem when students want to praise their God. All those who are refusing to allow these students to acknowledge the Father and the Son will one day bow down at the feet of God and His Son, Jesus, who they have refused on earth. For many, it will be too late, but I pray it will not. However, many have already bought into the trick of the enemy.

Philippians 2:9-11 (KJV)
9 Wherefore God also hath highly exalted him, and given him a name which is above every name:
10 That at the name of Jesus every knee should bow, of *things* in heaven, and *things* in earth, and *things* under the earth;
11 And *that* every tongue should confess that Jesus Christ *is* Lord, to the glory of God the Father.

Our fore-parents knew that in the United States of America, they could not do without God in their lives and country. Because they believed in God and knew who He was and still is in our country, they knew that home was not enough for their children to hear about the Lord God. Therefore, the Lord God was introduced in the school system so that the students will able to speak freely about Jesus and pray. There was some heathen in this blessed country who decided that the Bible and prayer do not belong in the school system, and they were successful in getting the court system to expel God from the schools. So, was it with Satan—he alone started this self-will behavior against God and caused other angels into disobeying God the Almighty One. A long time ago, it happened, and it is still going on, as you will find people just being a hater of Jesus Christ. Satan has used many of us as his advocate, as an instrument of dishonor to disallow the Bible and prayer in the schools through the decision of the court system. Some of the judges are no longer judging righteously anymore. God does not like unjust judgment; let us go back to the basic and start doing the right things, not pleasing those that have influences or money. As you judge, God also will judge your decisions.

Yes, I have come to understand that the school system is about the students, and they emphasized so much about students learning and safety. What about the students' spiritual protection in the educational system? Don't the parents have rights about which books are easily accessible to their children? I want to know this: since when books that have the content of witchcraft, which is of the devil, becomes part of students' education? The double standards and hypocrisy that are in this world. When sinners speak out about something that can hurt them, things change, but when Christians cry out for righteousness, they are considered to be a trouble maker and foolish. It's okay. Hell is waiting for many of us who refuse God and His son, Jesus Christ.

To the education system and businesses, do not let someone tell you that you should go against the Almighty God and His Son. Who do you think gives you the power to get wealth or the ability to do things of righteousness? All unrighteousness is of the devil and in the heart of humanity lieth wickedness. It is time that we come to our senses and realize that some of the things that we are doing are not working for us. Only Jesus Christ, the Son of the living God, can help us in our failures. Why not give Him a try?

Parents, what happened? We are so religious, but some of us are so blind. We are not standing up for our faith and the things that we believe in for the betterment of our children and ourselves. We fight and argue about sports for our children, but when it comes to Jesus, He is not that important. Jesus Christ is our hope in our school and business. Without Jesus Christ of Nazareth, you and I are absolutely nothing, zero. Less protest and more praying to God to change the hearts of the wicked. No human being can change the heart of another. Yes, we can influence a person to change their mind from doing something, but the thoughts are still within the heart. The problem in America and other countries is a heart problem. Haven't we heard what God who created us said about us in **Jeremiah 17:9-10**? But there is an answer to all of our problems, **2nd Chronicles 7:14-15.**

Parents, always pray for your children because you do not know what they may be doing when you are not around them. You do not know all of their friends. Pray for your children. Pray that they will know who's name to call on when troubles and problems stand in their way. This name is **Jesus.**

Jesus Christ is Lord, and no human being can ever change this truth because it was not a man who gave Jesus His name. When Mary was pregnant with Jesus, it had nothing to do with humanity; instead, it was all done by the Father and the Holy Spirit of God. Therefore, let us all as human beings know the truth and hold fast to it and not for one moment allow anyone to cause us to lose our faith in the entire truth of God, the Father, and the Lord Jesus Christ. The Father is the one who gave His son the name that rightly fits Him. *Amen*

CHAPTER SIX

Where does Jesus come from?

In the beginning "dateless past," God created the heaven and the earth. Genesis 1:1 (KJV)

Before **Genesis 1:1,** Jesus already was. Many people do not believe this is true. Please remember that the word of God is spiritually discerns. Therefore, we need the Holy Spirit of God to teach us the meaning of God's written words. Humanity does not know the things of God, regardless of how intellectual they are. If it was not for the Holy Spirit of God who gives us the revelation of God's words, we would know nothing.

John 1:1-5 (KJV)
[1] In the beginning was the Word, and the Word was with God, and the Word was God.
[2] The same was in the beginning with God.
[3] All things were made by him; and without him was not any thing made that was made.
[4] In him was life; and the life was the light of men.
[5] And the light shineth in darkness; and the darkness comprehended it not.

The word "**Word**" that is capitalized in the above verses is speaking of Jesus Christ, the only begotten Son of the living God. Before the heaven and the earth were created, Jesus already was, and He is also Lord.

The Father, "God," the Son, "Jesus," and the Holy Spirit made mankind according to the scripture in **Genesis**, yet many have come to hate the Maker of their spirit, soul, and body. These three individual parts make up a person.

Yes, the devil hates God, and he is a created being, but humanity is not a created being like the angels. Read the following scripture carefully. I truly believe that the only created part of mankind is their soul and spirit, but the body is made from the dust of the ground.

Genesis 1:26-27 (KJV)
26 And God said, Let us make man in our image, after our likeness: and let them have dominion over the fish of the sea, and over the fowl of the air, and over the cattle, and over all the earth, and over every creeping thing that creepeth upon the earth.
27 So God created man in his *own* image, in the image of God created he him; male and female created he them.

The God-head, which is also called the Trinity, made us in their image and after their likeness. Yes, every person is very special to the Father, and that is why Jesus, the Son, came and gave up His life for us so that we can be restored back to our heavenly place where we were supposed to be in the first place. If it were not for the fall of man in the Garden of Eden, we would be perfect forever.

Who is this man? His name is Jesus Christ, the Son of the living God. Adam was made from the dust of the ground and God-breathed within him the breath of life, and from the dust, man became a living soul. God gave the man a spirit, just like He God is a Spirit; we are like God, spirit, soul, and body. Jesus loves us very passionately beyond the ability in which our mind cannot comprehend such love. The scripture said that Jesus is also named Emanuel, which means God with us. When God came to us in the form of a man, whose name is Jesus, even though He was man, He was also God at the same time in the flesh, yet He was not in the fullness of His glory. Moses, when he came down from Mount Sinai, the children of Israel could not look upon him because the glory of God was upon him and his face was so shiny, that was the glory of God. It is the same with Jesus; if He came to us "mankind" in His fullness of whom He is at the time He walked on the earth, humanity could never come close to Him, and as a matter of fact, they would be overwhelmed because of His brightness. But Jesus came to humanity as a humble man to show us the way to the Kingdom of God by teaching us how to live a righteous and holy life that pleases and is acceptable unto God.

John 3:13 (KJV)

And no man hath ascended up to heaven, but he that came down from heaven, *even* the Son of man which is in heaven.

The verse above proves that Jesus was already in heaven before He came to us on earth. Many people refuse the truth, but they cannot change it, God's words will stand sure, and over the ages of time, the word of God has been tested, and it is still what it was sent out to do. No other writings have gone through what the word of God has gone through. The word of God is life, and it causes a change in people's lives, over and over again.

Our heavenly Father, "God," already knew what Jesus would have to go through and how He would be treated by mankind; even so, God allowed His Son to come because there was no other way for humanity to be saved from their sins. Jesus Christ is the Son of the Lord GOD, the Creator of heaven and earth, the only One who calls things forth, and they come into existence.

Jesus, the One who knew the beginning from the end of the earth, the men in those days, was not afraid to handle Jesus in such a disrespectful manner as they did back then and even now. I believe if Jesus were here on earth, many would treat Him the same and even worse. You may say, why would I say such a thing? What? Haven't you heard the news on the radio or see it on the television? We read about it on the internet and in the Newspaper, how the servants of God and His children are being treated as if we are their enemy. These people do not realize that when they abuse God's children in any way, they are also doing that to Jesus. There have been many, and even now, of God's children who are in prison. Why? Because they have acknowledged the call upon their lives to preach the gospel "meaning good news" and to inherit everlasting life of truth that Jesus Christ has commissioned them to do and to receive.

Even now, there are churches in the world that have been censored, and their mouth is muzzled from speaking about the love of their lives, and His name is Jesus. To those who are passing laws to restrain God's servants from delivering the message that Jesus gave them to be delivered, why would you do that? Are you the one that employed them to preach the gospel? Are you greater than God? Why have you allowed the devil to enter into your heart to put such a significant burden upon God's servants'? Because of your willingness to do the work of the devil, Almighty God will not hold you guiltless.

So, they treat us, the servants and His children, the Pastors and the believers, like we are their slaves, and they are the Master of our soul. Why? In their wickedness and ignorance, they are persecuting Jesus himself, not knowing it, but God will not hold them guiltless.

When you assign your subordinate to a task, you expect them to follow your instruction to the letter because you are their leader, and if he/she refuses, you may fire that person. Am I not correct about my statement? Well, God is greater than us, and He commanded us to go into the highway and byways and preach the gospel of Christ Jesus. Should we disobey Him? What is your answer?

In wickedness and ignorance, the Son of God was spat on, beaten nearly to death, and they put a crown of thrones on His head, constantly inflicting pain upon the Savior. They publicly hung Jesus upon a cross half-naked. We are talking about the Son of God, who is also Lord. They nailed His feet together onto the wood post and even His hands. Jesus Christ, the Son of God, hung on the cross for about six hours before He gave up His life for us.

The number six represents man. We can discuss that each hour that Jesus was on the cross represents the day humanity was made. Look at all that Jesus Christ, the only begotten Son of God, has done for all of humanity to deliver us from hell punishment and to be our Lord and Savior. We cannot be quiet; we cannot hold our peace; we must shout glory hallelujah to our King, who is the King of all kings and Lord of all lords. He is our only hope to receive eternal life, and all of God's children need to praise Him.

John 19:15 (KJV

But they cried out, Away with *him*, away with *him*, crucify him. Pilate saith unto them, Shall I crucify your King? The chief priests answered, We have no king but Caesar.

Mark 15:27 (KJV)

27And with him they crucify two thieves; the one on his right hand, and the other on his left.

Matthew 20:17-19 (KJV)

17 And Jesus going up to Jerusalem took the twelve disciples apart in the way, and said unto them,

18 Behold, we go up to Jerusalem; and the Son of man shall be betrayed unto the chief priests and unto the scribes, and they shall condemn him to death,

19 And shall deliver him to the Gentiles to mock, and to scourge, and to crucify *him*: and the third day he shall rise again.

Isaiah 52:14 (KJV)

As many were astonied at thee; his visage was so marred more than any man, and his form more than the sons of men:

Who is this man? This man Christ Jesus, who raised the dead, healed cripples, healed the dumb and deaf. Jesus even opens blinded eyes. He cast out devils from people that were possessed. He is a friend to the friendless, and Father to the fatherless, strength to the weak, rich to those who are poor, yet they crucified Him!

Who is this man? This man Jesus is the One that so many people love so dearly. We too love Him and honor Him and praise His holy name. Somebody, please tell us more about this man who is the author and finisher of our faith, and He who helps those that are helpless. Yes, the man Christ Jesus who was once dead. O glory hallelujah. And now He is alive forevermore. Praise the name of the Lord. Never again will Jesus die; you too, my brothers and sisters. And to all the unbelievers, the "sinners," if you will only accept the Son of God as your personal Savior and your life here on earth lines up according to the word of God, you will have life eternal.

Sinners, you must confess your sins, and He is faithful and just to forgive you of your sins. Not some of your sins, but all of your sins. Tell me more about this man Jesus, because we want to love Him more and more for our self too because there is none like Him. We want to give Him our whole heart, not a part of it, but all of it! Our soul must we give unto Him also our bodies.

1 John 1:9 (KJV)

⁹ If we confess our sins, he is faithful and just to forgive us *our* sins, and to cleanse us from all unrighteousness.

O Lord Jesus, take this life of ours, and our will and help us to conform to the **Will** of God the Father because we want to please Him in righteousness.

Where did Jesus come from? He comes from the Father in heaven, and Jesus went back from where He came to be with His Father in heaven. Jesus is waiting for the day when God the Father will say to Him, my Beloved Son, it is time to go and gather my people from the earth and carry all of them to heaven. Saints, what a glorious day that will be! We shall see Jesus coming from the Eastern sky in His glory to receive the church that He died for on Calvary. I pray that we will be ready. Do not let Jesus come and leave you behind. Whether dead or alive, brethren, we must work out our salvation with fear and trembling, knowing that the Holy Ghost is working on us so that Jesus will not find us with spots and wrinkles.

Brothers and sisters, we must not just love Jesus, but we must be in love with Him passionately because He too loves us so much it caused Him to be hung upon the cross on Calvary for all humanity. Brothers and sisters, it is not enough to say that you are a Christian; your lifestyle must reflect the meaning of the word Christian, Christ-like, or like Christ. Can all Christians truthfully say as they judge themselves that: "I know that my life is pleasing unto God, the Holy One who is in heaven"?

There is little fire in the churches on the earth at this present time. Maybe my statement is not correct, and if I am wrong, Lord Jesus forgive me for speaking that which is not correct. But we must admit most of the churches are not on fire for Jesus Christ. Where is the shout of glory hallelujah, praise ye the LORD God who sits on the throne? Most churches in this present day are timing the Holy Ghost by looking at the clock for when to finish the service and to go home. To do what? To fill our belly with food? Some of us take food as our god. May God forgive us lukewarm Christians for our selfish ways. Television also becomes a god to many (sports)!

Righteousness and Holiness

We need to get back to Holiness and Righteousness and back to the time when people truly loved the Lord.

We need to get some of the books that are in stores and read them, telling us about the lives of all those soldiers of the Lord Jesus and how they sacrificed their lives unto death for Jesus Christ. Many did not have the comfort of cars to travel; they rode horses for miles to preach the gospel in the winter and hot summer with not enough to eat. But these days we care so much for our comfort, many refuses to enter into the house of God where we should be to have a holy convocation; instead, they use television and radio for the church. There is a big thing going on now, and that is streaming on the internet. Please don't get me wrong, there is nothing wrong with this media, but they have their place. We must worship GOD, praise His holy name, exalt His name above all other names in this world, and lift the name of the only Savior of the world, Jesus Christ.

Children of God, let us take up the banner of Christ and move in the things of God and find our first love. Many of us have lost it or give it away. Be all that the Lord Jesus wants for us to be in Him to please the LORD God the Father. Many people are dying in their sin, and we, the Christians, children of the living God, are relaxing. We must witness to them unto repentance so that they, too, can have eternal life. May the LORD bless and keep all of His children in Jesus' name in all that we do in righteousness. ***Amen.***

CHAPTER SEVEN

Sanctification

What is sanctify or sanctification?

Example: When we surrender our lives to Jesus Christ and experience the new birth by the Holy Spirit, we are now born again. From that time, we are separate from the world unto God the Father for service into His Kingdom. Sanctify, or sanctification, is to set apart, after we are washed or cleanse with the blood of Jesus and the fire of the Holy Spirit.

Thessalonians 4:3-5 (KJV)
³ For this is the will of God, *even* your sanctification, that ye should abstain from fornication:
⁴ That every one of you should know how to possess his vessel in sanctification and honour;
⁵ Not in the lust of concupiscence, even as the Gentiles which know not God:

1 Peter 1:2 (KJV)
² Elect according to the foreknowledge of God the Father, through sanctification of the Spirit, unto obedience and sprinkling of the blood of Jesus Christ: Grace unto you, and peace, be multiplied.

Well, my brothers and sisters, all those who are called the children of the Highest, are you a vessel of honor separated unto God in Christ Jesus? Are you blameless from filthy lucre? Pastors, can your congregations speak well of you? I know that we are still in this flesh, and sometimes, if not all the time, the flesh wants to show off itself warring against our spirit. No matter what your weaknesses are in your flesh, are you telling me that your problems and or situations are bigger than the God that is in you?

How easily we do forget the truth or ignore the fact to keep ourselves sanctify. Let us, from this day, stop our excuses because some of us are putting the name of God's only begotten Son to shame whenever we sin as we refuse to live a sanctified life. Do we forget that the Lord called us to be holy?

Leviticus 20:7 (KJV)
⁷ Sanctify yourselves therefore, and be ye holy: for I *am* the LORD your God.

The Lord GOD is calling all humanity to be holy like Him. However, we know that not all will heed to the call that was given by our Father. We, the believers, must heed in obedience to what the Father asks of us to do if we are followers of Jesus Christ. What? What kind of God do we think our heavenly Father is? Do we believe He would ask or command us to do something if it were not possible? Yes, He knows that it is possible to live a holy life unto Him. If we are trying to do this of our self and strength, before we start, we have already failed. We have to live our Christian life in Jesus Christ through the power of the Holy Ghost that is living in every child of God.

It is the Spirit of God, "Holy Ghost," that will do the work in and through us. However, we must yield ourselves to Jesus, not a part of us, but everything that we got. Many Christians who consider themselves being a child of God do not believe in the working of the Holy Ghost and do not believe in the gifts of the Spirit of God.

Go ahead, mighty ones, that think that we, the children of the living God, can live a victorious Christian life in this wicked and sinful world without the Holy Spirit of God. We claim that God and Jesus live in us, which is true, but only by faith in Him through the Holy Spirit. Yes, they are in you, through the Holy Spirit of God, Father God, and the Lord Jesus Christ. They live in you by faith in them. Please do not make this Christian life so complicated; it is just this simple, only believe and put your **Trust** completely in God. We need to act on the promises of God and stop putting our **Trust** in man because humanity cannot keep your soul and heart clean.

Jesus Christ is in heaven right now, on the right hand of our Father, and He is making intercession on our behalf unto His Father and our GOD. The work that the LORD God and the Lord Jesus Christ are doing in us is always through the power and might of **His Holy Spirit.**

We must also thank Jesus for praying to the Father for sending us His Holy Spirit. We must thank Jesus for loving and caring so much for the children of God. He came to this earth to be with us and to comfort us. Therefore, Jesus prayed to the Father to send us another Comforter since He will not be with us in person, whose name is Holy Ghost. We must be very thankful to the Holy Ghost for the work that He is doing in us to glorify the Son of the living God.

John 14:15-17 (KJV)

16 And I will pray the Father, and he shall give you another Comforter, that he may abide with you for ever;
17 *Even* the Spirit of truth; whom the world cannot receive, because it seeth him not, neither knoweth him: but ye know him; for he dwelleth with you, and shall be in you.

John 15:26-27 (KJV)

26 But when the Comforter is come, whom I will send unto you from the Father, *even* the Spirit of truth, which proceedeth from the Father, he shall testify of me:
27 And ye also shall bear witness, because ye have been with me from the beginning.

It is full-time, brothers and sisters, for us to live a holy life pleasing unto God in Christ Jesus because Jesus is coming back for a Church without spot and wrinkles. If we obey the word of God completely, we will always please Him, and that is what He desires from us - obedience.

Ephesians 5:25-27 (KJV)
25 Husbands, love your wives, even as Christ also loved the church, and gave himself for it;
26 That he might sanctify and cleanse it with the washing of water by the word,
27 That he might present it to himself a glorious church, not having spot, or wrinkle, or any such thing; but that it should be holy and without blemish.

Children of God, are our lives blameless, meaning without fault? Can others speak well about us knowing that, that which they speak is a fact? Our speech must always season with truth and not lies; lying is of the devil, who is the father of all lies. We, as Christians, do not need to have any kind of association with the things that are not of God.

Christians should not be cursing by using foul languages at any time, and there should be no excuse for such behavior. Husbands, are you obeying the word of God concerning your wife? If you are, then you should not be treating her as if she is a doormat. If you are not, make sure you are not embarrassing her in public or even at home. If you are, then you should not be beating her (physically) as if you were disciplining a child when he/she done wrong. Jesus gave His life for all humanity, and we must appreciate Him for it because He loves us so much. Therefore, husbands, there should never be any reason at all why the husband should not treat their wife with great respect at all times.

It is about time that believers stop condemning the newborn Christians as if we are perfect in our ways. Haven't some of us also sinned with words and deeds at times? Therefore, when a baby (newborn) Christian sin or make mistakes, talk to them in love and pray for them. (*As my former pastor would say, the enemy preys upon God's children;*

therefore, we must not prey on each other, but rather, we must pray for each other in the name of Jesus.) As they seek God and grow in the things of their Lord and Savior Jesus Christ, the Jesus that is in them by the Holy Spirit will deliver them from the bondage of sin so that they do not get discouraged and turn back to the devil.

Believers, what has happened to some of us? Why are some of us Christians looking like the world? Have we easily forgotten what the scripture said, that we are supposed to be in the world but not of the world? **Sanctify thyself from the world system, and come out from among them and be ye different.**

James 4:4 (KJV)
⁴ Ye adulterers and adulteresses, know ye not that the friendship of the world is enmity with God? whosoever therefore will be a friend of the world is the enemy of God.

Some Christians are dressing like the sinful world, wearing shorts that are so short, like unto their underwear, and that's not modest dressing. No one should be seeing your brassiere and strap "bra." The dress code does not meet the godly standard of Christianity; women are supposed to dress and look like a virtuous lady. When the world sees you, they are supposed to see a difference in you and about you. They are supposed to see Jesus Christ in you at all times. The glory of God should be glowing upon you. Your walk is supposed to be different, and when you speak, your speech is supposed to be different from the world. When you go to the sanctuary to worship, you are to cover up yourself properly, stay away from skin fitted clothes because not everyone that comes to church is saved. Also, there may be members who are still struggling with the lust of the flesh in their hearts and your low-cut **V** neck blouse is not helping them. When you are in church and your clothing does not cover your knees, please carry something to cover up those legs' sisters. It is a fact, and it is a reality, and if you do not like it, take it up with the Holy Spirit.

1 Peter 2:9-10 (KJV)

[9] But ye *are* a chosen generation, a royal priesthood, an holy nation, a peculiar people; that ye should shew forth the praises of him who hath called you out of darkness into his marvellous light:

[10] Which in time past *were* not a people, but *are* now the people of God: which had not obtained mercy, but now have obtained mercy.

Some Christian men and women that are saved—that is, have surrendered their life unto Jesus and have faith in God— I do not doubt your faith, not at all. However, the ring that you are wearing on your tongue, what is that all about? Do you know why a person pierces their tongue? It is not everything that the unbelievers do that looks good or seems to be cute that is good for the children of God and His Son, Jesus. What is wrong with some of us Christians? Do you not know that we are a peculiar people, and whatever we do and say must be acceptable unto the Lord Jesus? Judge yourself, take a close look at yourself, and see if Jesus will be pleased with the way you look. We need to know and understand what **sanctifies** or **sanctification** means.

Ok, men, do you know the actual meaning of why men wear rings in their ears? I do not believe that men should wear rings in their ears in this present world and this is our opinion, mainly as a Christian. A pair of earrings in the ear of any lady is a decoration for them, but not necessary for men. However, it is not the same for the men, and it is a sign that you are a slave to a slave master, according to the word of God. Yes, we were slaves to the devil when we were in the world, pleasing him in the things that we do that was against the will of God, but now we are free by the blood of Jesus, and we do not need any earthly sign to signify that we are a slave or free-born in Christ Jesus. Our righteous lives are supposed to be the only sign of who we are. We are Christians, meaning we are Christ-like.

Exodus 21:6 (KJV)

[6] Then his master shall bring him unto the judges; he shall also bring him to the door, or unto the door post; and his master shall bore his ear through with an aul; and he shall serve him for ever.

Deuteronomy 15:17 (KJV)

[17] Then thou shalt take an aul, and thrust *it* through his ear unto the door, and he shall be thy servant for ever. And also unto thy maidservant thou shalt do likewise.

Christians who haven't yet had a tattoo or marking on their body should not put one on, but if you have tattoos already, just ask the Lord to forgive you in sinning against Him in ignorance. Please do not put any on your body. The scripture clearly stated that we should not put any marking on our bodies.

Leviticus 19:28 (KJV)

[28] Ye shall not make any cuttings in your flesh for the dead, nor print any marks upon you: I *am* the LORD.

We, as Christians, both men and women, must represent our Lord and Savior, Jesus Christ, in the way we adorn ourselves. Hello, what is wrong with some of us? We will do whatever it takes to please humanity; we dress ourselves to please them when we report to our job or a special occasion. There are dress codes that many companies have put in place for the workers to represent the company, and the employees are expected to follow the dress code, and if not, they will be reprimanded, written or verbal warning.

But when it comes to pleasing our King, King Jesus, some of us refuse to adhere to the code of dressing for Jesus their King. Some wear a tee-shirt to the sanctuary to worship the holy God, and I do believe that they can do better, but they have no reverence for God. Some wear shorts to the sanctuary to worship the holy God, and I think that they can do better, but they have no reverence for God. However, the Lord judges the heart and not the clothing. If the President invites you to the White House or the Queen of England invites you to Buckingham Palace, how would you dress for them? And they are just humans like you. But Jesus is God and deserves all the glory and honor.

For some Christians that do not care for the things of God, it is hard to correct them in the church; they are playing the world in the church, one foot in and one foot out, without the fear of the Lord God and His Son. Many Christians visit the club on the weekend and come Sunday, they seem to be the holiest ones in church. Christians, are you not fearful of falling into the hands of a terrible and just God? The word terrible does not mean that God is a tyrant, but rather, His judgments are powerful and righteous beyond our comprehension. Be very careful!

Christians let the world envy you, but you should not envy the world. Jesus Christ came not only to give you eternal life, but He also came so that we, the children of God, can have abundant life now. Do not look like the world, look different from the world. We are the ones that are supposed to inform the world and influence them how they are to look in their appearance. How can we judge when we are doing the exact things that the world is doing? The Bible says to judge with righteous judgment.

There may be some countries and States that recognize common-law marriages, but they lack knowledge of the word of God. They have allowed this to happen in their country or States, however, there is no such commandment from the Lord that is found in the Bible. God does not recognize common law marriage at all, it is either you are married or you are not. There is no such thing as common-law relationship, you made it up and it is not of God. Remember this; God has allowed marriages only between and man and a woman so that they will not have to sin against their own body and God. When anyone has sexual intercourse with another when not married according to the code of marriage that God alone set forth, it is a sin. The scripture said this:

1 Corinthians 7:2 (KJV)
² Nevertheless, *to avoid* fornication, let every man have his own wife, and let every woman have her own husband.

Ezekiel 18:4 (KJV)

⁴ Behold, all souls are mine; as the soul of the father, so also the soul of the son is mine: the soul that sinneth, it shall die.

Hate

Some people call themselves Christian and have hate within their heart for other human beings who God made in His image and after His likeness. Who are you to hate another human being? Are you telling the Almighty God that the people that look different from you, whether it is the color of their skin or from a foreign country of birth, that He has made in His image and likeness, is not approved by you? What, do you think that God has made a mistake? Who are you? Aren't you breathing the same air that God has given to humanity, or is your oxygen different from others? The statement above is not only for Christians but for all human beings.

God is love and full of love. He does not hate humanity in any way; however, some people hate others that God has made in His image and after His likeness. Christians, tell me which heaven you are going to when you have been prejudiced towards another person. Who gives you the right to hate when Jesus always reminds us to love one another? Because of the love that God has for humanity, He sent Jesus to die for us and to shed His blood for our forgiveness, and this was done for all humanity, and not for some; therefore, your hate for another person will take you into hell.

1 John 4:7-8 (KJV)

⁷ Beloved, let us love one another: for love is of God; and every one that loveth is born of God, and knoweth God.

⁸ He that loveth not knoweth not God; for God is love.

There is no hate in heaven, and if you died with hatred within your heart for someone just because they come from another country or they do not look like you, or their status in society, you are going to hellfire. Examine yourself with the word of God, and you will know if you are living according to the word of God. Are you sure that you are going to heaven where the loving God and His Son are? Loving a person does not mean that you have to tolerate their selfishness. Repent of your sin to God and live a life of love victoriously in Christ Jesus.

Fornication

When a person becomes a Christian, it means he/she is a believer in Jesus. We are like Christ. We are born again, not of the flesh but by the Spirit of God. We are now a new person because Almighty God washes us with the precious blood of His Son, Jesus, and now we are clean. If we should get this temple dirty again, it is all of our doings and not God. Nevertheless, God so loved us that He will forgive us if we would repent of our sins by opening our mouth and asking Him to forgive us. We now turn our back on the filthy things of the world. No longer should we be going around having sexual intercourse with others, except our wives and husbands. We have watch Nature program on the television, it was told and now we are knowledgeable of somethings. It is said that the Eagles does not mate with other Eagles, but they, male and female mate for life. Yet we, who are supposed to be more intelligent than them, are going around as if something has gone wrong in our head, spoiling young girls, leaving hurts, pain, tears, sadness and death behind us, because of our behaviors. The scripture said:

Deuteronomy 5:17-18 (KJV)
[18] Neither shalt thou commit adultery.

Exodus 20:14 (KJV)
[14] Thou shalt not commit adultery.

Please take exceptional notice of the above scripture under the law as the scripture said.

However, Jesus said this in the New Testament:

Matthew 5:27-28 (KJV)

[27] Ye have heard that it was said by them of old time, Thou shalt not commit adultery:

[28] But I say unto you, That whosoever looketh on a woman to lust after her hath committed adultery with her already in his heart.

No longer do we need to have sexual intercourse with a person that is not our spouse to be an adulterer, but if we only desire to have our neighbor's husband or wife in our hearts, we have already committed adultery in our hearts, that is what the scripture said. The Holy Spirit approved the writing of the scriptures, because He gave it to us from the Lord God, and we cannot change it to suit our fleshly desires. Many Christians may be saying that this is their body and they can do whatsoever they want to do with it. Oh no, not so! Your body does not belong to you! Who was it that molds this body from the dust of the ground and breathe life into it? It was God and not us. Neither is your Christian life yours. We are no longer our own; we were bought with a price, it cost Jesus, God's only begotten Son, His life so that we can now say "glory hallelujah, we have inherited eternal life" thank God for Jesus, we now inherit eternal life, and this life is in Jesus.

1 Corinthians 6:18 (KJV)

[18] Flee fornication. Every sin that a man doeth is without the body; but he that committeth fornication sinneth against his own body.

1 Corinthians 6:19-20 (KJV)

[19] What? know ye not that your body is the temple of the Holy Ghost *which is* in you, which ye have of God, and ye are not your own?

[20] For ye are bought with a price: therefore glorify God in your body, and in your spirit, which are God's.

1 Corinthians 7:2 (KJV)

[2] Nevertheless, *to avoid* fornication, let every man have his own wife, and let every woman have her own husband.

The Holy Spirit of God spoke the scripture to the Prophets and the Disciples; therefore, we must hold these scriptures precious to our hearts.

2 Timothy 3:16-17 (KJV)

[16] All scripture *is* given by inspiration of God, and *is* profitable for doctrine, for reproof, for correction, for instruction in righteousness:
[17] That the man of God may be perfect, thoroughly furnished unto all good works.

Sexual intercourse is only for married couples; nowhere in the scripture can anyone find where God said that sex is for singles. It is not there, so all of our justification is already proven wrong. Christians must have power over their own body and keep the temple of the Holy Spirit clean from filthiness. There are many things that the scripture does not list that we should not do; however, the information in the scripture has given us verses that cover so many elements of what to do and what not to do. The scripture reminds us that our body is the temple of the Holy Spirit. Because our body is the temple of God, this alone informs us that we should not do whatsoever we want to do in it and on our body, and it covers our excuses that because a Holy person is living within us as children of God. This Holy person within every Christian is Holy, Father, Son and Holy Spirit. Remember, God the Father and Jesus Christ the Son abides in us through faith in them, and the Holy Ghost "Holy Spirit" dwells in all believers.

Brothers and Sisters, Jesus did suffer for us in ways we can never imagine, and He died. Before He died, Jesus was hanging upon the cross for hours just because He loves humanity and in obedience to His Father in heaven. Jesus refused to come down from the cross because love holds Him there. And thank God that the Lord Jesus stayed on the cross because if He did not, the human race would be lost forever. Jesus, in His obedience, accomplishes the work on the cross. Therefore, we as Christians need to be obedient to God for the work that Jesus did on the cross for our sinful soul.

The scripture said that all believers must flee fornication. Are we obeying the word of God? Imagine this, if every single person abstains from fornication. *First,* they will not sin against God and their own body, and when we sin, we need to ask God right away to forgive us in Jesus' name.

Second, there will be no more unwed mothers and unwanted pregnancy. Through abortions, so many young adults are destroying the life of their babies. Some women and young girls throw away their babies as in throwing garbage in the trash bin, by having abortions by the millions and killing them for what reason. The government and the court system have given doctors the legal right to kill or murder the child that is within the womb of that mother. Also, the mother has hired the doctor to take a life. Are you sure of what you are doing? Do you genuinely think a heart to heart consideration that Jesus approved of what you are doing? *Third,* they will be a significant turnaround of sexually transmitted diseases that are so devastating to the lives of young people throughout the world, spreading germs from person to person, causing many to suffer, and so many have died. The wages of sin are death, and when we refuse to obey the word of the living God, death is lying at our doors. When we sow to the flesh, we will reap corruption in our body; therefore, Christians and unbelievers, flee from the sin of fornication and all other sins.

Christians, children of the living God, stop running around doing these things that you used to do while you were in the world. Yes, we are in this world, but we must not be a part-taker of the ungodly things of the world. Many elements of the world are of unrighteousness, and all those that are called the children of God should not be partakers of those things because it puts the precious name of our Lord and Savior Jesus Christ to shame. Do you want to shame the name of Jesus? No, well, stop it!

Stealing and Cursing

The scripture said that we are not to steal any longer because we are children of the living God. We must guard our mouth, no cursing or words of profanity, idle words, or gestures.

James 3:9-10 (KJV)
9 Therewith bless we God, even the Father; and therewith curse we men, which are made after the similitude of God.
10 Out of the same mouth proceedeth blessing and cursing. My brethren, these things ought not so to be.

Ephesians 4:28 (KJV)
28 Let him that stole steal no more: but rather let him labour, working with *his* hands the thing which is good, that he may have to give to him that needeth.

We must not steal from our neighbors anymore. We must not steal from our employer anymore if you use to do it before. Your Father in heaven will provide for your needs. Will it get hard at times, yes, but we must put our **Trust** in God by faith and at no time waver. However, we must line up with God's plan for our lives so that we can inherit the riches that God has for us in Christ Jesus. Nevertheless, He said that He causes the rain to fall on the just and the unjust.

There are some Christians who are still going around cursing as if they have not experienced the new birth. Well, have you? Why is it that some Christian's life is just like the unbelievers? Children of God, you must be teachable. Those who are still living after the flesh, you need to go through deliverance so that you can be delivered from the strongholds of disobedience in your life.

Greetings, my Christian brothers and sisters, what is that you have in your mouth that looks like a cigarette? What! Haven't you heard what the word of God said that your body is the temple of the Holy Ghost?

Christians have no legal right to smoke any kind of cigarette, cigars, or marijuana, period. Cigarettes cause illnesses that can leads to lung disease within the body. To the saints that are smoking, do you want the Holy Ghost to dwell in the temple that is full of sicknesses that could be prevented? You must call on God to help you stop smoking so that you do not have to destroy your body by smoking, and you must mean it and believe in your heart that as you asked the Lord to take away the taste from your lips that He will do it in Jesus name.

UNBELIEVERS: Do you really and truthfully believe that cigarettes help you calm down and stop your nervousness. It is not the cigarettes that are helping you, but rather, it is the chemical compound that is in them that your body becomes addicted to. Jesus can help you stop smoking if you choose to ask Him for help. Jesus loves you just as He loves all those who choose to be His followers. Jesus' help is just a call away. He will never be too busy to listen to you and come to your aid, but you must open your mouth and talk to Him. You can also get help from the servants of the living God, the pastors in counseling.

Many unbelievers are afraid to come to Jesus because of the life that some Christians are living. They do not see Jesus in those Christians. Yes, another person's life has nothing to do with another person's salvation. Still, we are the reflection of the Son of God, and we must be cautious that we do not cause others to sin in ignorance because of our behavior. Yes, each person has to know Jesus for themselves; however, the Christian life should be so holy and pure that those who are in the world want to have what God's children have.

Your holy worship and praise that you sent up to God our Father, in the building "the sanctuary" or "church building" on Sundays or wherever we gather together to have a holy convocation, should also reflect who you are when you leave the sanctuary. Nothing should change beyond the four walls; our lives are supposed to be a reflection of Jesus Christ, the only begotten Son of God at all times.

Children of God, let us from this day stop our foolish and ungodly behavior and call on God in Jesus' name to change our heart, mind, and life so that we can please Him who died for our sins.

Children of God, we may not have everything in this world; nevertheless, we know that we will receive of the Lord our crowns at the appointed time in Christ Jesus. This crown is not made with man's hand; our crowns are in heaven waiting for the time set forth for us to receive it or them. Most important, the crown is just a reward, but our eternal life is the most important thing that any child of God can ever receive.

Christians, we are children of the Highest. The Lord is His name who owns the entire Universe, and we are the ones that are supposed to own many of the wealth in the world, but some of us have been taught differently. We are supposed to be the lender and not the borrower; we are supposed to be the giver and not the receiver. Something is wrong with our financial conditions, and we must fix it today and not tomorrow. We must line up with the things of God for our lives so that we can receive direction from our heavenly Father in the manner that we must live, for us to receive from Him the good things of the world.

The enemy is fighting for our soul, and we must fight back in prayer to keep it in the name of Jesus, for it is only Jesus who has overcome the enemy. He won the victory for us on the cross, and our fights are not natural but spiritual. Jesus already defeated our chief enemy, the devil, who is always working, trying to cause us to sin against the Sovereign One - God Almighty. Remember this, the devil never takes a day off; he works seven days a week, twenty-four hours a day. He is never tired of making trouble for us, but we will always win if we only follow the prescription of the word of God.

James 4:7 (KJV)
[7] Submit yourselves therefore to God. Resist the devil, and he will flee from you.

Christians are special

Christians, we are a peculiar people, and we are unique in the eyes of God, and this profession that we have taken up is eternal. Therefore, we must crucify this flesh daily so that we can win at all times in Jesus' name. God wants the very best for His children; however, do we, the children of God, like the very best for ourselves? Ok, you feel frustrated, but you are not defeated if you are still living for Jesus. Fear and doubt will let you feel like that, but as Christians, we must get rid of the fear that is in our lives so that we can focus and be a winner and live a life of victory in Jesus' name. And if you fall from grace, what are you doing down there? Are you going to stay down for the rest of your life and refuse to get up in Jesus' name and conquer the enemy that you have allowed to cause you to be where you are today?

Get up in the name of Jesus Christ through the power of the Holy Spirit of God and start living again for God, so that God can glorify His Son, Jesus, through you, the vessel of honor. When sinners condemns Christian, remember this: Almighty God does not condemn you because you are His.

Now, if so, it is full time that we as Christians walk the walk of faith, talk and speak the words of righteousness, and always doing the things that please our God. No more dance hall party! No more drunkenness! No more taking of illegal drugs. No more busybody from house to house carrying and bringing tales. Your heart should be full of love in Christ Jesus. Make the fruit of the Spirit a part of your daily life.

1 Thessalonians 4:7 (KJV)
[7] For God hath not called us unto uncleanness, but unto holiness.

Colossians 3:5-7 (KJV)
[5] Mortify therefore your members which are upon the earth; fornication, uncleanness, inordinate affection, evil concupiscence, and covetousness, which is idolatry:

⁶ For which things' sake the wrath of God cometh on the children of disobedience:

⁷ In the which ye also walked some time, when ye lived in them.

Mortify: *to put to death or become dead to.*

All believers of Christ Jesus must put their flesh to death from these things that are causing us to sin. No longer should sin rule our body. Yes, we can and must put away all those things that dishonor God.

Romans 6:11-14 (KJV)

¹¹ Likewise reckon ye also yourselves to be dead indeed unto sin, but alive unto God through Jesus Christ our Lord.

¹² Let not sin therefore reign in your mortal body, that ye should obey it in the lusts thereof.

¹³ Neither yield ye your members *as* instruments of unrighteousness unto sin: but yield yourselves unto God, as those that are alive from the dead, and your members *as* instruments of righteousness unto God.

¹⁴ For sin shall not have dominion over you: for ye are not under the law, but under grace.

Fornication: *The act of a harlot, having sexual intercourse between two persons who are not married.*

Uncleanness: *Foul or dirty. Morally defiled. Ceremonially impure. Physical and moral uncleanness.*

Inordinate affection: *Excessive passion one toward another. Lust.*

Evil concupiscence: *A strong desire. Sexual desire. To lust after something that are forbidden.*

Covetousness: *Excessively and culpably desirous of the possessions of another. Eager for gain. Extortion.*

What the Apostle Paul is telling us here through the Spirit of truth is that before we become children of God, we use to walk in the way of unrighteousness after the things of the world. But now we are children of the living and holy God, and we are saved through the death and shed blood of His Son, Jesus. No longer should we put the name of the Lord to shame by doing uncleanness in our body.

Children of God, we are now the light of Jesus in the world. Do not, for one moment, let the filthiness and greed of this world cause any one of us to sin. In those things mentioned above and even more, they do not honor and glorify the Lord Jesus.

We are children of God, and we must act like we are children in obedience to our heavenly Father and the Lord Jesus Christ. God loves us so much that He gave us His Son. Therefore, from this day forth, let us start living a life that is pleasing and acceptable unto Jesus Christ, for when we please Jesus, we also please the Father. Jesus came to give us life, so let us appreciate the life that God gave to us through His Son, Jesus.

John 10:10 (KJV)
[10] The thief cometh not, but for to steal, and to kill, and to destroy: I am come that they might have life, and that they might have *it* more abundantly.

The churches lost their values

Many believers have misquoted the scripture where Jesus said to come as you are. Jesus was not telling us to come as we are in the way that we dress; instead, He was talking about the condition of our hearts and lives.

When we are sick, do we wait until we are better to go and see the doctor? When you are better or get well, there is no need to go to the doctor except for our annual checkup. It is the same with Jesus. He was not calling those who are righteous, neither did He came to save the righteous but the unrighteous to salvation. The Lord Jesus came to heal the brokenhearted, to set the captive free, and to lose those that are bound in Satan prison. Even now, Jesus is still calling the unrighteous to righteousness. Jesus is calling the sick, lame, and the disease who are in sin for a checkup in His office since He is the Great Physician, and the Holy Spirit is waiting to operate on all of us to cut out the tumor of sin. Sin is like cancer; it spread throughout your body and life.

Jesus is calling those who are lost in sin to come unto Him and He will give them life. All need salvation and cleansing of their soul from all unrighteousness. This calling is for all human beings because all were born in sin. Jesus was not speaking about the way that we need to adorn ourselves to enter into His courts with praise. Jesus is not slack in His ways and manners, He set examples for us, but some churches have lost their values in many ways of following Jesus. Many churches now look so much like the world. I do not know why some pastors have allowed slackness to be in the house of God. We need to help and guide the flock, but we must remember who is our leader.

Jesus said that the house of God is a house of prayer, not a house of entertaining slackness. I have come to understand that there are some church members wearing pajamas to church services. What! Have we lost our minds? We have compromised the word of God and what the sanctuary is supposed to be. Would you look like this for your leaders of the world? You know, I stand corrected, because of money, some work place uses the term dress-down and wearing pajamas to raise money for some project. Should we have to lower our standard because of money? We have also entertained homosexuals and lesbians in the church holding leadership positions. With the agape love in my heart for the Lord Jesus Christ, I must take a stand: pastors, this ought not to be, realign your church ministry before the judgment of God come and judge you and the guilty ones.

Jesus is the head of the church. Pastors and members, do we not fear the Almighty God who is so holy that even the doorpost move at His presence? The scripture said this:

Philippians 2:12 (KJV)

[12] Wherefore, my beloved, as ye have always obeyed, not as in my presence only, but now much more in my absence, work out your own salvation with fear and trembling.

When a person trembles, this act of trembling is for a moment, or it goes and comes. However, when someone is trembling, it is constant. This is what we are asked to do: we should work out our salvation with constant fear, judging ourselves to make sure that we please the Most High God, the Sovereign One, and His Christ.

It is not just about clothing; nevertheless, how we adorn ourselves in the house of God is vitally important. Humanity is so quick to do anything to please one another, but when it comes to pleasing God, we would rather compromise His will for our will. Aren't we fearful of the wrath to come upon the generation of the disobedient? Some of this is happening with many of the young people in the world. Too often, young people are not respecting their parents. They are disobedient, not honoring their parents. Some of them seem to be ruling the household, leading them down the road of destruction, and the parents partly have to be blamed. Mothers, who carried that child in the womb for all those months? Did they give birth to you, or did you give birth to them? Take a stand in your home and instill values in your children's lives so that they may live long upon the earth according to the scripture.

Ephesians 6:2-3 (KJV)

[2] Honour thy father and mother; (which is the first commandment with promise;)
[3] That it may be well with thee, and thou mayest live long on the earth.

I pray that parents will stop acting as if they and their children are the same age and start training them in the way of the Lord God and Jesus Christ, the Savior of the world. The scripture said that disobedience is as the sin of witchcraft. Christians, do you not love your children? Hell is real. Do not let them destroy their lives because we think that they have to be pacified. Love them, but at the same time, be very stern with them.

Look good at all times for the King of all kings' and the Lord of all lords', Jesus the Savior of the world, but most importantly, make sure that your life is pleasing Him who is perfect and holy. ***Amen.***

Special request to children

Ephesians 6:2-3 (KJV)
2 Honour thy father and mother; (which is the first commandment with promise;)
3 That it may be well with thee, and thou mayest live long on the earth.

Colossians 3:20 (KJV)
20 Children, obey *your* parents in all things: for this is well pleasing unto the Lord.

The above scriptures are strictly for all children, and they are to be taken very seriously so that you can please Him, who gave the commandments. Children, the Lord has commanded you to honor and obey your parents so that you may live long on the earth. Children, are you following the commandments of the Lord?

So many parents have worked so hard to make sure that their child or children have shelter over their heads, food to eat, clothing on their body, and so many other things that they would need for their comfort. Many children are very unappreciative (ungrateful) to their parents for all that their parents have done for them. Some parents know that they cannot afford to give their children some of the things that they asked for, but yet they put themselves in debt and provide it to them. So many parents have done all that they could for their children, but the rewards that they receive are frustration, pain, disappointments, and headache.

Some parents have failed to grow or train their children in the prescribed manner, which the Lord has told them to; they are supposed to be trained and nurtured in the fear of God and to respect you and others. They are supposed to be taught to respect themselves, families, neighbors, and strangers, and also to obey the word of God. You are supposed to train them up to respect you without having to compromise your duties as parents. Parents, your children cannot be your friend; it is impossible. It cannot be, and it will never be so, no matter how hard you try to make it so. Mothers give birth to the child; therefore, you are the parent and that child is your child. Mothers and fathers, some of us have caused our children to violate the promise that the Lord has given them. You are causing them to cut their lives short on this earth because they do not honor anyone of you.

Children, whatever it is that your parents ask you to do, do it because they are your parents, and you must obey them. Except for two areas, if your parents want you to break the natural laws or to sin against God, then you must answer them in a very respectful manner why you cannot do it. Children, no matter what your parents say or do that is wrong, you must still show them respect. Parents may not always be right, but they must be respected at all times. Remember, children, you must respect your parents at all times and pray for them to be a better parent if they are not.

Children, please follow the following statements below, do this so that the Lord can forgive you for the way you have treated your parents over the years. Go to your parents and apologize to them for the way you have disrespected them and mean it from your heart and ask them to forgive you.

1.   Tell them that you are sorry for all the times you shut the door in their faces.
2.   Tell them that you are sorry for all the times you cursed them when you did not get what you wanted, not knowing that they could not afford to give it to you.
3.   Tell them that you are sorry when they refuse to let you sleep over your friend's home, not knowing the reason behind the 'no' answer.
4.   Tell them that you are sorry when they told you that you cannot bring girls or boys in their home to sleepover under the same roof when you are not yet married, and you curse them out for guiding you correctly.
5.   Tell them that you are sorry when they really could not afford that lunch at a particular fast-food restaurant.
6.   Tell them that you are sorry for abusing them physically when you raise your hands and hit them.
7.   Tell them that you are genuinely sorrowful for all the hurt, pain, and disappointment that you have caused them over the years.

These are just some things that I thought of. You know what you have done wrong, go to them and make things right with them so that the Lord will bless you.

Children, you know all that you have done to your parents that is not right. The above lists are just a few. After you have apologized and asked your parents to forgive you, then you, in turn, forgive your parents for anything that they may have done or said to you that hurts you. Because if you do not forgive them, neither will your heavenly Father forgive you of your wrong. After that, you need to ask God to forgive you for the way you have treated your parents.

Parents, I know that some of your children are out of control, but there is hope in Christ Jesus. Why not rededicate them to God in prayer who gave them to you and whose children they all are. Parents, the Bible said this:

Ephesians 6:4 (KJV)

[4] And, ye fathers, provoke not your children to wrath: but bring them up in the nurture and admonition of the Lord.

Colossians 3:21 (KJV)

[21] Fathers, provoke not your children *to anger*, lest they be discouraged.

I pray that every home will seek the face of the Lord and ask Him to give their family the peace that passeth all understanding in Jesus' name.

CHAPTER EIGHT

Pastor's woe unto you and us

Grace, mercy, and peace be unto all the servants of God in Christ Jesus our Lord and Savior. And unto all those who are called children of God, may the peace of our Lord and Savior, Jesus Christ, that passeth all human understanding, rise in you today.

Jeremiah 23:1-2 (KJV)
[1] Woe be unto the pastors that destroy and scatter the sheep of my pasture! saith the LORD.
[2] Therefore thus saith the LORD God of Israel against the pastors that feed my people; Ye have scattered my flock, and driven them away, and have not visited them: behold, I will visit upon you the evil of your doings, saith the LORD.

This chapter is about the nation of Israel, but it is also relevant in these present days because many pastors are not taking care of God's children, the flock, as we should, and the Lord is not pleased with us. We were employed by the Lord God to preach the gospel of Jesus Christ and Him alone.

Pastors, God is not pleased with some of us who refuse to feed His sheep the proper way and cause many to be scattered into the world among wolves. Yes, you have been fed by the Almighty God with the treasures from heaven that God has given unto you for His sheep, but some are not preaching sound doctrine. Remember this very carefully, pastors, the flock, they are not yours, they are God's.

Was it you that suffered and died on the cross at Calvary for the sins of humanity? No, it wasn't you. Well, feed the people with the word of God. It was Jesus' blood that was shed for the washing, cleansing, and remission of humanity's sins. No, it wasn't yours. Well, feed the people with the word of God. Was it you that went into the depths of the earth and took the keys of death and the grave, setting free those that were in captivity by the devil? No, it wasn't you. Feed the people with the word of God. Who was it that God raised from the dead by His Spirit in three days? And now He that was dead is alive forevermore, and His name is Jesus. No, it wasn't you. Well, feed the people with the sound doctrine of the word of God.

Pastors, many of us are refusing to preach or teach the word of truth, "Sound Doctrine," as the Lord Jesus has commissioned all of His servants to do. But instead, so many are preaching compromising gospel because they do not want to offend anyone. Oh, you do not wish to offend anyone? But when they end up in hell because you refuse to preach the gospel of truth, what can you do for them then?

Matthew 10:35-37 (KJV)
35 For I am come to set a man at variance against his father, and the daughter against her mother, and the daughter in law against her mother in law.
36 And a man's foes *shall be* they of his own household.
37 He that loveth father or mother more than me is not worthy of me: and he that loveth son or daughter more than me is not worthy of me.

Mark 16:15-16 (KJV)
15 And he said unto them, Go ye into all the world, and preach the gospel to every creature.
16 He that believeth and is baptized shall be saved; but he that believeth not shall be damned.

Jesus did not say that the servants of God should compromise the preaching of the gospel to His children. The word of God is the sword of the Spirit.

Ephesians 6:17 (KJV)
[17] And take the helmet of salvation, and the sword of the Spirit, which is the word of God:

Hebrews 4:12 (KJV)
[12] For the word of God *is* quick, and powerful, and sharper than any twoedged sword, piercing even to the dividing asunder of soul and spirit, and of the joints and marrow, and *is* a discerner of the thoughts and intents of the heart.

For too long now, some of God's servants fail to declare the word of the living God unto His people so that they can line up with the plan and purposes that God has for their lives. So many of God's children are feeding in dry and thirsty land in the church that they are in, because there is no food there. We must get the Holy Ghost back into the church so that His fire can burn again. There is no food (Sound Doctrine) in the pasture (church) that they are in, meaning "the churches and the word."

When the word of God is preached, souls should be convicted and lives change, unless the people refuse to accept the message. When the people resist the gospel that is delivered to them, they, in turn, reject the word of God and the Lord Jesus Christ because they refuse the sword of the Spirit.

Pastors, you are not chosen by the Lord Jesus to please everyone in the preaching of the gospel that the Holy Ghost has entrusted you with to deliver. If you preach the gospel, people will talk; if you refuse to teach it, people will talk; therefore, declare, thus saith the LORD God unto His people, about His Son. Something is very wrong when so many people proclaim that they are Christian and the fruit of their lives is not bearing righteousness.

Two reasons, either they are not saved or because they do not know how to live a Christian life. Some people are not reading the scripture for themselves; they depend on their pastors to tell them everything, what to do and what not to do. Many pastors are not preaching or teaching sanctification. There are many Christians who do not know how to live a life pleasing and acceptable unto the Lord Jesus Christ, and they need to be taught.

Some Christians believe the life that they are living is a life that is pleasing and acceptable unto Jesus Christ. They need to be taught the meaning of the cross and all that Jesus has done for them.

Christians, do you want to know how to live your life on this earth successfully for Jesus? Read the Epistles of the Apostle Paul. There is no lacking of knowledge and wisdom when you read his writings that were approved by the Holy Spirit. Everyone will experience a significant gain of understanding in all the epistles of Paul's letters. However, children of God, you need a good study Bible to have a better understanding of the cross of Jesus, primarily what the Apostle Paul writes about the cross of Jesus Christ in the book of Romans.

Please read and study the entire Bible; you will come to grow in the things of God when you start to study the word of God for yourself. I must thank my God for my Pastors who teach: ***What does the Bible say?*** By showing the truth in the scriptures and not humanity's opinion, everyone will benefit if they are willing to learn.

Christians, stop being so lazy and pick up the word of God and read it for yourself so that you will know if what is preached by the pastors is true or not. To those pastors who are preaching heresy for so long, stop it, repent and get back on track because God will not hold you guiltless for deceiving His people.

2 Peter 3:15-16 (KJV)

[15] And account *that* the longsuffering of our Lord *is* salvation; even as our beloved brother Paul also according to the wisdom given unto him hath written unto you;

[16] As also in all *his* epistles, speaking in them of these things; in which are some things hard to be understood, which they that are unlearned and unstable wrest, as *they do* also the other scriptures, unto their own destruction.

When a couple has children, it is their responsibility to train their children to be respectful to themselves and others. The parents also must start teaching their children how to write and count even before they start daycare and so much more. There are some things that some parents will not able to help their child or children with because some things are too hard or complicated; therefore, those children would need someone who is trained to teach them.

Okay, pastors, are you not like a natural parent? However, in this case, you are the spiritual parent to God's children here on this earth, and they must be taught by you in the things of the Almighty God. Jesus has called you to work for Him, preaching and teaching the word of God that was given unto Him by His Father.

Pastors, I know that there are many Christians who called themselves a child of God, and they are so sensitive to the words that you, the pastors, preach. Someone on the job or even their supervisor will mistreat some of us Christians because we need the job for the money, and if there is no money coming in, the bills and other things will not be taken care of promptly. Most of us will take the abuse at the workplace from the uncircumcised lips of the unsaved person, yet you get offended by the word of truth from the pastors.

Yes, pastors, we must know how to speak to God's children, because there is always a right and a wrong way to do things and how to speak. Nevertheless, at no time should a preacher or teacher of the gospel allow some sensitive child of God to cause them not to let the Holy Spirit of God minister through them to bless the children of God.

By the way, pastors, we are not self-employed to the profession of faith to preach the gospel, but it is the Lord Jesus Christ who called us to work in His Vineyard. Was it not God that employed you to preach and teach this glorious gospel of redemption? I do hope that we remember we are called to work for the Sovereign One, and it is such a great privilege to work for the most excellent employer of the universe. Let us for a moment look at the church as a corporation.

Mankind

There are two kinds of churches; first, the spiritual church, and secondly, the visible church. The church that Jesus established upon the rock is the corporation. God is the head of all things, and He is the **CEO** of the Church, His people. Jesus Christ is the **Overseer** of the Church of God, and the Holy Spirit is the **Supervisor.**

In every cooperation, the **CEO** and board members that are formed help chair or run the business; they come together and write policies and procedures to protect themselves from liabilities; with this said policies and procedures, it is to protect the company and workers of such company.

Jesus

Well, the Trinity has done the same. The Holy Bible is the policy and procedure manual that God has given to His Son, Christ Jesus. In this Holy Manual, there is information that if the workers in the Kingdom of God read it and understand what is written, it will protect them from hell through Jesus, the Overseer.

The Holy Ghost is the Supervisor who is here on the job—never taken a day off and twenty-four-seven supervising to make sure that the work of God is carried out decently and in order, and that the employees are protected from harm and danger from the devil.

Mankind

Yes, there are some workers of the company that will not like what the company policies and procedures are, and many times some companies have changed their policies and procedure to please individuals or groups. Many times, when there are compromises, something goes wrong, and many times it can cause the company not to function as effectively. The **CEO** depends upon the supervisors and all the managers to help make the company successful by their conduct and knowledge of their job requirements.

Jesus

The Holy Bible is the road map to the Kingdom of heaven in the Kingdom of God. In this book, God has given to all humanity the procedures, policies, and directions of His Kingdom. He will never for a moment change any word to please humankind; what is written is written and cannot be changed. Some pastors are promoted by the **Overseer**, "Jesus," and approved by the **Supervisor** "Holy Ghost," and some of us are changing the written policies and procedures that the **CEO** did not give any of them the authority to change. They have taken upon themselves the power to change God's word without any regard for what the Lord said in His words. Presumptuous are they, and they have no fear of the Lord. Only the Lord has the right to change His laws and covenants. The **CEO**, "GOD," who has given this gospel to His Son, Jesus, the **Overseer**, said this:

Revelation 22:18-19 (KJV)

[18] For I testify unto every man that heareth the words of the prophecy of this book, If any man shall add unto these things, God shall add unto him the plagues that are written in this book:

[19] And if any man shall take away from the words of the book of this prophecy, God shall take away his part out of the book of life, and out of the holy city, and *from* the things which are written in this book.

Pastors, do not change the word of God to please anyone so that you can make friends with them or get more money on Sundays. Why would God give it to you for them if He wants the word to be changed? The Holy Bible is not the Constitution of any nation, in which if someone does not like something in it, they can change the writing to please people. Yes, some things may be changed, but not to destroy the foundation of truth that the nation was founded upon. There are no Amendments in the Bible; if need to be, the Holy Spirit will do it at His will, but since there is no change that is required, the word of God stands because His word is established in heaven. Only Jesus was allowed to make any kind of Amendment to the word of God, and He did not change the concepts; He makes them more transparent for us to understand; therefore, it was not a change.

Matthew 5:17 (KJV)

[17] Think not that I am come to destroy the law, or the prophets: I am not come to destroy, but to fulfill.

Preach the written and living word of God under the power of the Holy Spirit, so that the Father will get the glory, and Jesus Christ will be exalted among us on the earth. The gospel is about Jesus and all that He did for the children of God and for those who have not yet come to accept the truth about Jesus Christ as Lord and Savior. When the gospel is preached, it will bring the result one way or another. It will cause people to change their lives.

Pastors, some of us are not allowing the Holy Spirit to move in the church services so that the anointing will break the yokes and destroy the works of Satan that are upon the people. Pastors, preach the gospel to the people of God so that God will get all the glory and Jesus Christ be exalted among us on the earth, and sinners will be convicted and surrender to Jesus, crying out for the forgiveness of their sins. The gospel is supposed to inform sinners that only one person can forgive their sins, and that person is Jesus. The gospel is supposed to encourage the saints to know that fellowship with Jesus is not in vain, and if they continue serving God, they will have eternal life.

The gospel is to inform all of us what Jesus has done for us on the cross at Calvary: how He loved us so much that He gave His life as a ransom for us so that we may live forever. The gospel is to be preached and inform God's people how to live for Him by serving Him in holiness through sanctification. The gospel is good news, and it needs to be told so that Christians and sinners will come to the knowledge of the precious blood of Jesus and what His shed blood means for them. Pastors, may God continue to bless and keep you and your families as you continue to work for Him in His Vineyard.

Numbers 6:24-26 (KJV)
[24] The LORD bless thee, and keep thee:
[25] The LORD make his face shine upon thee, and be gracious unto thee:
[26] The LORD lift up his countenance upon thee, and give thee peace.

Amen

CHAPTER NINE

What did it cost?

It cost God's Son, Jesus Christ, His life for our salvation.

1 Corinthians 6:20 (KJV)

[20] For ye are bought with a price: therefore glorify God in your body, and in your spirit, which are God's.

When we are washed and purged with the precious blood of the Lamb of God and the fire of the Holy Spirit, we are no longer our own, we belong to Jesus Christ. We are bought for a very high price, and all the money in the entire world could never pay for one person's sin. All the blood sacrifices that were done in the Old Testament could never cause a person sins to be washed away, but rather, it was their obedience to God that saved them until the precious blood of Jesus was shed for their sins and ours. The blood sacrifices in the Old Testament times were just an example of the perfect sacrifice to come, and it has already arrived. Jesus was crucified on the cross at Calvary for our disobedience. He shed His blood for all of humanity's sins so that we can be forgiven of our sins by our heavenly Father, God. The Old Testament Saints could never go to heaven except for two that the scriptures mentioned:

Genesis 5:24 (KJV)

[24] And Enoch walked with God: and he *was* not; for God took him.

2 Kings 2:11 (KJV)

¹¹ And it came to pass, as they still went on, and talked, that, behold, *there appeared* a chariot of fire, and horses of fire, and parted them both asunder; and Elijah went up by a whirlwind into heaven.

All of the different kinds of animals and birds that were sacrificed could never save anyone. That is why the Old Testament Saints were in paradise, which was under the earth, according to scripture, and not far from hell until Jesus took them to heaven.

Luke 16:26 (KJV)

²⁶ And beside all this, between us and you there is a great gulf fixed: so that they which would pass from hence to you cannot; neither can they pass to us, that *would come* from thence.

Even when Jesus was here on earth before the resurrection, they were still in captivity; why is that? Because the precious blood of Jesus was not yet shed to free them from captivity. The blood sacrifice of the animals and birds could never wash anyone's sins away, neither was it a permanent covering for their sins, and to make an atonement. The LORD God allowed a temporary cover with the blood of animals and birds. It also foreshadowed the precious blood of Jesus.

However, when the perfect One, Christ Jesus, the Lamb of God, shed His blood on the cross for the atonement of our sins, Jesus offered up His blood to God for us. God's only begotten Son shed His blood so that we, the New Testament believers, do not have to sacrifice any animals or birds for our sins. Jesus already sacrificed His life; therefore, we do not have to kill a sacrifice because Jesus did it all for us once.

We, the New Testament saints, need to believe by faith what Jesus has done for us on the cross. We need to have faith in the cross, not the wood that Jesus was crucified on, but rather, what He has accomplished for us; He paid it all in full for us and that is why we owe God all the glory, honor, and praise for what His Son did for all of us. The blood of Jesus Christ is so pure and potent against sin that Jesus only need to sacrifice His life once, which he did. There is so much power in the blood of the perfect Lamb of God, and that is why His blood washes and cleanses all of us who come to Him for repentance. His precious blood covered us, and God took away our sins so that when the LORD God looks upon us, He sees no blemishes, only vessels of honor. Now that we have received the washing by the blood of Jesus, we are to be careful to keep the temple clean because the Holy Spirit of God is now living in our body, which is called the temple.

1 Corinthians 3:16-17 (KJV)

[16] Know ye not that ye are the temple of God, and *that* the Spirit of God dwelleth in you?

[17] If any man defile the temple of God, him shall God destroy; for the temple of God is holy, which *temple* ye are.

1 Corinthians 6:19 (KJV)

[19] What? know ye not that your body is the temple of the Holy Ghost *which is* in you, which ye have of God, and ye are not your own?

None of us have the legal right to sin in our body, neither do any of us have the legal right to do whatever we choose to do with our body because we are not our own.

Jesus paid a great price for humanity. The sad thing is that not all mankind is willing to receive this perfect gift from God, the Father. God will not take back this gift that He has given to us. To lose this gift, we are the ones that give it back to God. This gift is the person of Jesus and the life that is in him, eternal life.

Think about these events very carefully. Children of the living God and all the unbelievers who have not yet asked Jesus to come into their life. God sent His only begotten Son, Jesus, so that He can give His life for ours, which He did. Now, how is it working for you? Are we still running around in this world doing the things that do not please God?

What sound are we listening to? Where are we going? Are we still going to the dance hall, and if yes, what are you looking for there? Have you gone back into your old ways, walking up and down on the earth like the devil, looking for something that does not benefit your Christian life? We are now a new creature, and we must make sure all that we possess in our body, home, and life are pleasing to the Lord.

Do we truly understand what Jesus did for us on the cross? On the cross, Jesus suffered much for humanity. The cross is so important for us humanity, because if the death and shedding of blood was not done humanity would be lost forever. The act on the cross saves humanity from the wrath to come and the everlasting punishment in hell, and to reconcile humanity back to God. Jesus needed to go to the cross and suffer for us. Because God loved us, He gave us His Son, Jesus, **St John 3:16**. God, the Father, has foreknowledge of the heart of man; God knew that they would kill His Son Jesus, that He sent unto us to save all humanity from their sins, but the price that was needed for our sins has to be perfect and costly, and no one else could do this for mankind. Please note that God already knew all that would happen to His Son, Christ Jesus. No one could have paid for their sin, because we are not perfect like Jesus, the only lamb without blemish.

Jesus suffered so much within His body for all of us before He died. Mankind spat in Jesus' face. Several times the scripture tells us that they tried to stone Him. He was ridiculed for all of us. They bound Him and beat Him so severely that it was hard to recognize Jesus. They nailed His hands and feet to the cross. They pierce His side with a sword. All of this He went through just because God and His Son loves us.

Matthew 27:2 (KJV)
² And when they had bound him, they led *him* away, and delivered him to Pontius Pilate the governor.

John 18:12 (KJV)

12 Then the band and the captain and officers of the Jews took Jesus, and bound him,

Jesus' hands were bound as if He was a criminal. What crime did Jesus commit? If loving people who were made in the image and likeness of God is the crime that Jesus was guilty of, then He is guilty of loving us. Because of His love for us, He came to do the works that His Father has given Him to do. Jesus did that which His Father asked Him to do without complaining. What did Jesus do? He brought to humanity salvation by grace, and this salvation contains all that mankind would ever need in this earth to inherit the Kingdom of God.

They beat Jesus nearly to death. No matter what they did to Jesus, He could not die. If they stoned Him, He could not die, even though He was so severely beaten. He could only die upon the cross. The cross is the death that God chose for His Son to die for the sins of all mankind; no other death would be accepted by the Father; humanity was a curse; therefore, when Jesus hung on the cross, He became a curse for us.

Isaiah 52:14 (KJV)

14 As many were astonied at thee; his visage was so marred more than any man, and his form more than the sons of men:

Children of God, it cost Jesus, the Son of God, His life unto death for all humanity. We, as Christians, must be like Christ and desire to have the mind of Jesus Christ. Yes, this world is not friendly to Christians, but we must remember what our Lord and Savior has already told us about the world. Let us love each other as our Savior has commanded us to do and keep one another in prayer because we are all Christians, they are our brothers and sisters in the Lord. Please remember to pray for the unsaved love ones in our families, co-workers and friends.

Amen

CHAPTER TEN

Homosexuality

James 1:13-16 (KJV)
¹³ Let no man say when he is tempted, I am tempted of God: for God cannot be tempted with evil, neither tempteth he any man:
¹⁴ But every man is tempted, when he is drawn away of his own lust, and enticed.
¹⁵ Then when lust hath conceived, it bringeth forth sin: and sin, when it is finished, bringeth forth death.
¹⁶ Do not err, my beloved brethren.

Leviticus 18:22 (KJV)
²² Thou shalt not lie with mankind, as with womankind: it *is* abomination.

When Christians talk against homosexuality, those who are in that lifestyle believe that Christians hate them because of the lies that they have been told and think of themselves. Gentlemen and ladies, we love you, that is why we are telling you the truth. If we did not love you, we would not tell you the truth, but those that are encouraging you to go on, they do not love you, or maybe they too are blind and cannot see for themselves. How can a person see someone in fire and does not try to help them from burning? We have known of a fire that is getting ready to burn you and all that sin, and only Jesus Christ that can prevent you from burning in this fire, but you must turn away from your lust.

Many of us hate the truth, but the truth is of God. Christians do not and should not hate anyone other than sin. When people refuse to make corrections, they come up with different excuses and lies about those who are doing the correcting according to God's word.

Humanity is not the one who inspired the writing of the Bible. The Word of God said that the Spirit of God is the One who does that; therefore, the words that are contained in The Holy Bible are true, and it cannot be changed and will not be changed by God to please sinful people. When the scriptures speak clearly about the indecency of this lifestyle and that it is wrong, what is the fuss all about? God said it is wrong, then it is wrong, and that's it. If anyone has any logical sense of reasoning within their mind, there is no need to debate the written word of God. The word of God is not just a written word from God, but the word of God is alive, and it is a law, and it reflects the mind of the Lord. I encourage you to read ***Romans 1:20-32.***

I have come to understand that there are government officials who are trying to shut the mouth of the pastors who speak out about this sin. It can be considered to be a hate crime whenever someone talks or preach against such un-Christ behavior. All those government officials who are quick to pass law contrary to the word of God need to consult with the servants of God before they go ahead and pass laws that are very controversial in this country. The word of God is never contentious. Some people try to make the truth of God controversial because their hearts are full of sin. You, the lawmakers and judges who are going against the word of God and passing a law that men can marry men and women can marry women, know this: you are also guilty of this sin, and there is a fire that is burning and none of us can extinguished it. Know this, there is a place in hell waiting for all that have sinned and come short of the glory of God and His Son, Jesus Christ.

America is a great country, and we need to stop following other countries that have lesser moral values. What works for some countries does not necessarily mean that it is suitable for this country based upon its Judeo-Christian foundation. The people of this nation need to stop this foolishness and come to the understanding that the pastors are doing the work of God, and the Lord expects us to preach the gospel of Jesus Christ without compromising, regardless of who it may cause to be uncomfortable. The word of God should not and must not be compromised at any time for anyone. When the ungodly speak against the pastors and try to threaten them by vomiting poisonous words from their mouth against the servants of God and God's children, they do not realize that they are attacking the Lord Jesus Christ.

Through the word of God, I have come to understand that humanity is beneath God and some mankind dares to try to tell God that what He has said in His word is not true, especially those who are in power. Many are trying to bribe God's servants not to obey their Master's voice, wanting us to compromise the meaning of the written words of God just because some people will be offended and their feelings get hurt because of truth; know that hellfire will burn them more. I do not want to go there, neither do I wish for anyone to go to hell; because of our disobedience, many will end up in hell to be punished according to the scripture. Haven't you heard what the word of God is supposed to do? The scripture tells us that the word of God is sharper than any two-edged sword.

Hebrews 4:12 (KJV)
¹² For the word of God *is* quick, and powerful, and sharper than any two-edged sword, piercing even to the dividing asunder of soul and spirit, and of the joints and marrow, and *is* a discerner of the thoughts and intents of the heart.

To all those who are passing laws to quiet the churches of the Lord Jesus Christ, please stop it. It wasn't you who died for our sins, and it wasn't you who shed your blood on the cross for the forgiveness of sins. It was the Son of God who suffered greatly for humanity. He shed His blood and died for all of us, and we turn around and spat in His face presumptuously.

Yes, we must use wisdom, and we must also be wise as a serpent and harmful as a dove. This does not mean that Christians should let the ungodly do whatever they want to do to us and whenever they choose. Children of God, we are not praying as we ought to, to our God and Father in heaven. We are not praying against this sin as we must; instead, we find many "Christians" who are living the lifestyle of homosexuality. If you do not change, hell will open up her mouth waiting for you. Who has bewitched you and told you lies that it is okay to glory in the passing of laws that men can now marry other men and women can do the same? No, please do not glorify because you do not know and understand what they have done against this Nation by passing this law. This act is against nature, and it is an abomination to the will of God.

They have caused this Nation to sin against God like this Nation may have never sinned before in history since this country become a country of Christian liberty.

"I rebuke and bind the spirit of Sodom and Gomorrah and all uncleanness from this country in Jesus's name."

Some pastors are also engaging in this lifestyle too, and that is why there is such a compromise in the pulpit. Those who are real Christians and living their life to please God and His Son will not compromise their relationship with their heavenly Father. We love the people, but the act of their sinful behavior we just cannot tolerate. The law is all man-made law, and it comes from the pit of hell, and it is not God's law. Therefore, thus saith the LORD God, I will visit your Nation in due time, and I will cause you to be sorrowful when the stench of your abomination reaches my nostril. To the officials, please understand this and try not to forget it. We are Christians, and we must obey God's standards for our life on this earth, not a compromised one. When God said to do this, that is precisely what God meant and nothing else. God means what He says and says what He means.

Sir/Madam, when you asked someone on your staff to do something for you, you expect them to carry out your assignment(s). If you did not expect them to do it, why did you waste your time to ask? The laws that are in this country are expected to be followed. That is why laws were passed to govern in the first place. When the laws are broken, the one who breaks your precious law is found guilty.

Well, God, who is above all of us, has a more excellent law for His children and all humanity. When Jesus commanded His Apostles to go and preach the gospel to the nations, that also meant preaching against the lifestyle of homosexuality so that they too will be saved and have eternal life. We must obey our Master and Lord because He is above us and He is God. Why are you passing laws for people to sin against God and end up in hell? What about you? I am sure some of you are praying at night asking God to forgive you so that you will not die in your sins, but for politics and long career, you are doing a great disservice to the citizen of your country.

Christians, do not preach hate and should not preach hating another person that God has made; we should and must always preach the salvation that God's Son brings to us, and this salvation includes many benefits. Please read the Bible and come to know the truth.

One more thing to the officials, if you will read and study the word of God for yourselves, you will come to understand that God is telling all of us human beings how to live our lives here on earth to please Him in every way. Also, the penalty for disobeying the Lord is very severe because the sentence is everlasting; there will be no bail, no, not even parole. Most importantly, I pray that you will give your life unto Jesus. When you become a believer, you will start to see things God's way and not man's way because right now, you are very blind.

I do not have any hate in my heart for anyone throughout the entire world because my God commanded me to love all people. We were all made in the image and likeness of Jehovah God. But He never commanded us to tolerate wickedness and things of the world that can cause someone to go to hell. Whenever anyone openly speaks out against homosexuality, they are considered to be hateful. It is also considered now to be a crime when anyone talks or preaches against such a lifestyle in some countries. What? Are all these people ignorant about the truth of hell? Why they would think of such a law? God is using us, His people, to minister to sinners so that by hearing the word of God, they will have faith in Jesus Christ of Nazareth and He will save them from their sins before it is too late. But those who pass laws are not helping; instead, they are actually hurting these people by defending and encouraging unrighteousness. Some lawmakers are supporting bills that are not godly to please people so that they can continue voting for them to be in Washington. Washington D.C., be very careful of brimstone and fire, it is coming. Washington D.C. is in serious trouble, Washington needs Jesus Christ's presence because Washington is on their way to hellfire, not all but most. Why? Because of all the lies and corruption. Hypocrisy, hate shown between others, and poison coming from their mouth against those who God created in his image. They spoke and kept others up in their hearts. Many pretend to care for the citizens of this country, but they seem to care more for the money and their positions; if you truly care, remember the citizens and not yourselves. Almighty God is watching you and hearing all that you are doing and speaking in secret. Is there someone that God can use to change Washington D.C., when that person comes forth, you will be hated because of the change for the betterment of the citizens of this country, and other's.

When we talked or preached against homosexuality, it is not that we hate these people, but rather, it is the lifestyle which is sin that they are committing within their body that is abominable. First, God at no time hates anyone; He just keeps on loving all human beings. It does not matter who you are or where you come from, Jesus loves you, and if He did not love and cares for you, He would not have died for you. That is why He came and died for our sins. Yes, it is always the sin in our lives that God cannot love. Repent and worship God and live.

Mark 12:30-31 (KJV)

³⁰ And thou shalt love the Lord thy God with all thy heart, and with all thy soul, and with all thy mind, and with all thy strength: this *is* the first commandment.

³¹ And the second *is* like, *namely* this, Thou shalt love thy neighbour as thyself. There is none other commandment greater than these.

Leviticus 20:13 (KJV)

¹³ If a man also lie with mankind, as he lieth with a woman, both of them have committed an abomination: they shall surely be put to death; their blood *shall be* upon them.

We are all God's children from the seed of Adam and Eve. Because they sinned, all human beings are born in sin. Because we are born in sin, all human beings need a Savior to save them by forgiving us of our sins, and this Savior is Jesus. Many refuse to listen and obey Him; Jesus came to save all of us from our sins. Why don't you obey and follow Him today?

Mankind is made in the image of God and after His likeness. We have come to hate sin in our lives, and those who failed to change and die in their sins will eventually go to hell. Christians should not hate people, only the act of sin, because we know what it will cost us if we do not change. When we say Christian, we are referring to those who believe in Jesus Christ, and they are spiritual born by the Holy Spirit.

Many people on this earth do not believe that there is a real place called hell, and this place was made for the fallen angels and Satan. There is no other place that God has prepared for the punishment of disobedient people because it was never the plan of Almighty God to send humanity to hell. Some people really and genuinely do possess wickedness within their hearts, and this would be the place for them, like the devil and the angels that rebel against the Creator of heaven and earth with the false prophets.

To all those people who are living this lifestyle of homosexuality, you need to stop this ungodly behavior before it is too late for you. When you die in a state of sinfulness, you will go to hell. It is just that simple yet true. We always speak about hell and forget to remind them that are living in sin, and that their final destination is the lake of fire.

"What does the Bible say"?

Revelation 20:10 (KJV)
[10] And the devil that deceived them was cast into the lake of fire and brimstone, where the beast and the false prophet *are*, and shall be tormented day and night for ever and ever.

Revelation 20:14-15 (KJV)
[14] And death and hell were cast into the lake of fire. This is the second death.
[15] And whosoever was not found written in the book of life was cast into the lake of fire.

Revelation 20:15, Yes unbelievers, this is where you will go if you do not accept Jesus Christ as your Lord and Savior. When you accept Jesus as your Savior and live your life to please Him in all your ways, He will write your name in the book of life. But, if you reject Jesus Christ, then in the lake of fire, you shall go.

Humanity is not your enemy; the devil who is deceiving you is your enemy. You have allowed him to come and trick you into believing lies, just as he did to Eve. Come on, people, you do not need to go to a University to figure this thing out. It is not healthy for men to have a sexual or romantic relationship with another man and the same for the women. It is downright wrong and immoral. This behavior is not healthy, it is ungodly, and there is hope for you, but only Jesus can help you get rid of that which motivates you through the power of the Spirit of God. The blood of Jesus will wash you and make you clean.

Our enemy, the devil, as the scriptures inform us, will one day be cast into the lake of fire. The other scripture said that both death and hell will be cast into the lake of fire. You do not have to end up there. Stop listening to those who are encouraging you to continue living this ungodly lifestyle. They are not helping you; instead, they are hurting you more than you can ever imagine. I am encouraging you to seek life in Jesus Christ. They are telling you to go ahead and live as you choose, then die in sin and go to hell while they make it in heaven, then hell and death will be cast into the lake of fire, with you and them.

Because God loves you so much, He sent His only begotten Son, Jesus Christ, to come and suffer the pain of sin for you in His body. Now you can be free from this sin. Because God loves you, Jesus Christ died on the cross so that you will be free from this bondage of sin, and you will never experience the second death, which is the eternal separation from God.

Because God loves you, He allowed His Son, Jesus, to shed His blood on the cross at Calvary so that the blood of Jesus can wash away your sins and the Holy Father "GOD" can look upon you not as a sinner, but as His child, because of what His Son, Jesus Christ, has done for all on the cross. All those who accept Him will have everlasting life. Yes, there are many people out there who are lying on the true and living God, the Holy One, who is the Sovereign One. In Him, there is no unrighteousness or blemishes. Jehovah God calls us to be holy for He is holy.

Officials pass laws allowing people who are living the lifestyle of homosexuality to be married as husband and wife of the same sex. Are we mad? How can anyone in their right mind believe that it is ok to pass such a law in this country as if it is a reasonable thing to do? This is unnormal and it comes from hell. If you think it is so good, leave your darling spouse and join them. But you won't because you know how wonderful it is for a man and a woman to be together. Hypocrites, many of us are!

Keep jumping for glory because your name is on a bill that is heading for the pit of hell; you have not seen glory as yet. Wait until you see the Son of God coming in His cloud of glory when you shall bow down and worship Him. Jesus Christ of Nazareth is our King, and He is above all other kings. Jesus will sit on His throne to judge humanity for the sins that we have committed while living on the earth. All of the people whose names are not found in the book of life will be cast away from His presence because we refuse to obey Him. Not because of homosexuality but because of the sinful life that we chose to live before we die. Consider what you have gotten yourself into because of your fleshly desires. Turn around and change in the name of Jesus Christ, and let God cleanse your mind and heart so that you can also have eternal life which is in Jesus only. You will never find everlasting life in another here on earth; anyone who says otherwise is a liar.

I have heard that some make the statement that they were born feeling different in their body, that who they are is not what they're supposed to be. Man becomes attractive to men and women the same. Yes, it can happen, but it is not from God; it is from Satan, the devil, through the sinful nature that is within every human being. The sinful nature in you comes alive within any one of us to choose to do good or evil. However, God did not and could not create anyone that way. If it were true, then the Lord God would not speak out about these distasteful ways. Their spirit and soul as a baby were always perfect until birth. At the age of accountability is when we recognize right from wrong and understand what we are doing. Furthermore, the only other valid scenario to explain why a person says that they were born that way is because a familiar spirit of sexual perversion input this feeling in them while they were in their mother's womb. Parents pray for your babies and ask Jesus to cover them with His precious blood. Demons are real and they go about looking for available bodies to live in, pray until you pray, and when you think that you have prayed, pray some more.

God did not and will not make a person(s) be a homosexual individual. The LORD God is against such behavior. Why would the Holy God ask of us to be holy like unto Himself and, at the same time, cause you to sin against Him? The Lord will not cause you to live in this state of abominable sin because He is holy. Whatsoever state that a person dies in, in that very state of sin, he/she is sealed until the day of judgment. This lifestyle is of the devil; it comes from the pit of hell, including all unrighteousness. When we find ourselves to be ungodly and unholy, it is not of God, it is because of our carnal mind. It is full time we take responsibility for our actions and stop blaming others.

Another thing is this: it does not matter whether you are practicing homosexuality or not, anyone that dies in sin will be judged for the sins in their life. According to the word of God, all souls that sin will die. This death is the second death. The first death is the physical death that we all must experience because of sin; however, the second death is the eternal death in hell, and the final place will be the lake of fire, because we refuse to accept Jesus Christ as our Savior and Lord.

Revelation 21:8 (KJV)

8 But the fearful, and unbelieving, and the abominable, and murderers, and whoremongers, and sorcerers, and idolaters, and all liars, shall have their part in the lake which burneth with fire and brimstone: which is the second death.

2 Thessalonians 1:8-9 (KJV)

8 In flaming fire taking vengeance on them that know not God, and that obey not the gospel of our Lord Jesus Christ:
9 Who shall be punished with everlasting destruction from the presence of the Lord, and from the glory of his power;

Our enemy, the devil, has always tried to pervert the holy things of God. He is a liar, and he will always be a liar. God said that sexual relationship is for couples, meaning a man and a woman, and they are to be wife and husband. The enemy makes it seem as if it is okay for singles to have sexual relationships knowing that such conduct is ungodly, and if anyone died in such a state, they too will be in hell.

God's will for humanity is to restore all back to their rightful place just as when Adam and Eve were in the Garden of Eden. There they had a perfect union with God until they sinned. The devil is trying all that he can do for all to be in hell with him, experiencing everlasting punishment like himself. He will not stop until he somehow tries to fill hell with humanity. We are very dear to the heart of the living, truthful, Almighty God, but we must obey Him who is holy.

Remember this, and do not forget that God made all humanity in His image and likeness, and Satan, our enemy, does not love anyone of us. He hates all people. Satan is a thief, a killer and a liar, and so much more. All that is bad comes from the devil, and because of him, the world is in the condition that it is facing right now, but all the blame should not lay on him because we were instructed to resist him and he will leave us. It is not the devil that causes anyone to do what they have done; it is a person's choice to do what they want to do. The devil never forces a person's hands to do evil. We are the ones that allowed evil to enter into our hearts, and out of the soul precedes wickedness under the influence of Satan.

John 8:44 (KJV)

[44] Ye are of *your* father the devil, and the lusts of your father ye will do. He was a murderer from the beginning, and abode not in the truth, because there is no truth in him. When he speaketh a lie, he speaketh of his own: for he is a liar, and the father of it.

John 10:10 (KJV)

[10] The thief cometh not, but for to steal, and to kill, and to destroy: I am come that they might have life, and that they might have *it* more abundantly.

Luke 9:56 (KJV)

[56] For the Son of man is not come to destroy men's lives, but to save *them*. And they went to another village.

The devil is a liar from the beginning. He lied to Eve by telling her something different from what God has said. And he is still telling lies by using deceptions in the lives of those who allowed the devil to use them or that individual to dishonor themself. Jesus did not come to destroy lives; He came to save the lives of all those who want to be saved. The person who comes to save or to help those in need can only do so when they arrive at the scene. When a person comes to help someone, who is in a death situation, the rescuer can only help that person who is in need if they are conscious and with their cooperation to rescue him or her. If the person is unconscious, that is different. The person that is in need to be saved must allow the rescuer to pull him or her to safety.

God sent His only begotten Son into this world to save humanity and get us to safety. Some of us do not want to be saved, and we resist the rescuer. Instead of looking onto the only One that can save them from their condition and or situation, they refuse the help. God will not force Himself on anyone. God gave all of us free will to choose and many have chosen life to live and not die; however, many are still refusing to accept the Savior of their soul.

Jesus Christ is the only One that can save a person from the lifestyle of homosexuality. It is not a sickness that can be cured by any doctor. Even though the act is physical, behind the scene it is spiritual warfare. Many may say it is a disease. If It is a disease, where is the cure for it? There is no physical cure for the act of homosexuality because it is not a physical condition. It is spiritual, and only the spiritual acts of righteousness can warfare against the spirit of darkness to lose that person's mind from bondage. Therefore, only God can deliver all from their sins in the name of Jesus Christ. Many people in this world are in Satan's prison, their mind is locked up in darkness, and only Jesus can set them free from this prison. The prison that they are in is the prison of bondage, Satan's stronghold, possessed by demons that are associated with Satan. Those that are in bondage can be free from the prison of sin that the enemy has them in, but they must accept Jesus Christ as their Savior, or they are prayed for and under the anointing power of the Holy Spirit can they receive deliverance even if they are not yet save.

The Christians

Many of us profess that we are a believer of Jesus "born again by the Spirit." When a person is born again, that means that they have repented of their sins, made Jesus Christ their Lord and Savior, washed with the blood of Jesus Christ, and purged with the fire of the Holy Spirit. At this time, they are now Christ-like; they are now a follower of Jesus. In Jesus, there is no darkness, only light. Therefore, when a person accepts Jesus, the darkness that was in them is now gone. The light of Jesus is now in them, and that light is Jesus. What do light and darkness have to do with each other?

You cannot be born again and be practicing this filthy, disgraceful, ungodly lifestyle. You just cannot do it; it is as simple as that. It is not all about homosexuality, it is about sins in our lives. Yes, you may love the Lord; however, the spirit that is in you needs to go out of you in Jesus' name. Read the Bible, and you will see that God is against this behavior. All homosexuals and lesbians out there, Jesus loves you, and He died for you, and He shed His blood for you so that God will forgive you of your sins. But you need to have a mindset to call out to Jesus and ask Him to help you turn away from this ungodly lifestyle so that you, too, can inherit the Kingdom of heaven.

Genesis 19:1 (KJV)

¹ And there came two angels to Sodom at even; and Lot sat in the gate of Sodom: and Lot seeing *them* rose up to meet them; and he bowed himself with his face toward the ground;

Genesis 19:4-5 (KJV)

⁴ But before they lay down, the men of the city, *even* the men of Sodom, compassed the house round, both old and young, all the people from every quarter:

⁵ And they called unto Lot, and said unto him, Where *are* the men which came in to thee this night? bring them out unto us, that we may know them.

Genesis 19:7-8 (KJV)

⁷ And said, I pray you, brethren, do not so wickedly.

⁸ Behold now, I have two daughters which have not known man; let me, I pray you, bring them out unto you, and do ye to them as *is* good in your eyes: only unto these men do nothing; for therefore came they under the shadow of my roof.

Genesis 19:13 (KJV)

¹³ For we will destroy this place, because the cry of them is waxen great before the face of the LORD; and the LORD hath sent us to destroy it.

Genesis 19:24-25 (KJV)

²⁴ Then the LORD rained upon Sodom and upon Gomorrah brimstone and fire from the LORD out of heaven;

²⁵ And he overthrew those cities, and all the plain, and all the inhabitants of the cities, and that which grew upon the ground.

Romans 1:26-28 (KJV)

²⁶ For this cause God gave them up unto vile affections: for even their women did change the natural use into that which is against nature:

²⁷ And likewise also the men, leaving the natural use of the woman, burned in their lust one toward another; men with men working that

which is unseemly, and receiving in themselves that recompence of their error which was meet.

[28] And even as they did not like to retain God in *their* knowledge, God gave them over to a reprobate mind, to do those things which are not convenient;

Brethren, in these evil times that the world is facing, we need to get closer to God and His Son, Jesus Christ. We are living in the last days, and because of it, we will see things get deteriorated continually. The above scriptures teach us that those who choose to live a life of ungodliness in homosexuality have consequences that will befall them in life—spiritual or natural—if they do not turn away from such. In the name of Jesus Christ of Nazareth, God will judge you for the deeds of these abominable acts if you continue in this sinful lifestyle. God will also judge those lawyers and politicians who have helped pass laws declaring homosexuality legal as if it is a natural thing to do. It is wrong, and it will always be wrong.

James 4:17 (KJV)

[17] Therefore to him that knoweth to do good, and doeth *it* not, to him it is sin.

What God has said about our ungodly behavior, be it known that He will not change His mind. The word has gone out; all souls that sin will die. But it does not have to be. Jesus came to save all those who sin. All our sins will be forgiven and will be cleansed with the blood of Jesus Christ, except for one, and that is blaspheming against the Holy Ghost.

The elected politicians who are passing laws permitting same-sex marriages do not love you. Neither do they care about your spiritual life because if they did love you, they would not for one moment encourage you to do something that is wrong and against the word and the will of God. Why would they think this is ok? What do they have to gain by being on your side to favor you in doing that, which is an abomination?

Jesus loves you; this is why He is correcting you. He loves you so much. He was willing to die for you to save you from this sin and all others. It is not too late for you to turn around; there is hope in Jesus. The only time your hope is lost forever is if you or anyone else died in sin.

Can any of these people that are passing laws for you to continue doing what you are doing take you out of hell? Can they advocate for you against God when He sentences you to everlasting punishment in hell? They may have the power and authority here on earth to pass laws to protect and continue this immoral behavior, but man does not have the power and authority to send someone to heaven or hell.

Let us learn from the experiences of those in the scripture. It is too late for the fallen angels; they joined the enemy of God and rebel and they are sentenced to everlasting punishment by God. The men and women of Sodom and Gomorrah knew how terrible the grip of this type of sin is on someone's life, especially when they are in it for a long time. Do not reach the place of not knowing right from wrong by being a reprobate.

All those who are Christians and are partakers of this lifestyle, examine yourselves and turn away from this ungodly lifestyle before it is too late for you. The scripture said, by their fruit, they shall be known. What fruit are you bearing? Is your fruit the fruit of righteousness?

Matthew 7:16 (KJV)
16 Ye shall know them by their fruits. Do men gather grapes of thorns, or figs of thistles?

God can use the devil to draw someone closer to Him to save someone's soul from sin. Does this mean that the devil is saved or righteous? No! All of us, by now, should know this as it is written. Satan will never have eternal life with the Lord in heaven or on earth. He is sentenced to the lake of fire. What! Is this life of sin so precious to you that you are willing to suffer the pain of sin while here on earth and then to be a cast away for eternity?

God used men and women to preach the gospel, meaning good news, but that does not imply that all are saved. Many of them were called to work for God, and then they turned away from the faith, doing what they want to do just like you. Many, for some reason(s), have allowed the things of the world to draw them away from the faith. Now and then, Christians do and say things that displease God, and this means that they have sinned; however, it does not mean that they are sinners. A sinner is a person who fails to accept Jesus Christ as their Savior, who is the only begotten Son of GOD. A sinner is a person who refuses to change from their old ways to the new direction in Jesus Christ. Many have accepted Jesus Christ but turned away from the faith in Christ to go back into the world to involve in sinful behavior, whom they once knew. Obey the word of God and live.

Pastors and children of the living God in Christ Jesus, through the washing of His blood, judge yourself and see if you are bearing the fruit of righteousness. Are you Christ-like in all your ways?

Psalms 82:2 (KJV)
[2] How long will ye judge unjustly, and accept the persons of the wicked? Selah.

1 Corinthians 11:31-32 (KJV)
[31] For if we would judge ourselves, we should not be judged.
[32] But when we are judged, we are chastened of the Lord, that we should not be condemned with the world.

The scripture said that we should judge ourselves and come to see and know the unrighteousness that is in our lives so that we, as Christians, can immediately ask God to forgive us in the name of His Son, Jesus. The scripture also said this:

Ezekiel 18:31-32 (KJV)

[31] Cast away from you all your transgressions, whereby ye have transgressed; and make you a new heart and a new spirit: for why will ye die, O house of Israel?

[32] For I have no pleasure in the death of him that dieth, saith the Lord GOD: wherefore turn *yourselves*, and live ye.

Jeremiah 23:23-24 (KJV)

[23] *Am* I a God at hand, saith the LORD, and not a God afar off?

[24] Can any hide himself in secret places that I shall not see him? saith the LORD. Do not I fill heaven and earth? saith the LORD.

Jeremiah 17:9-10 (KJV)

[9] The heart *is* deceitful above all *things*, and desperately wicked: who can know it?

[10] I the LORD search the heart, *I* try the reins, even to give every man according to his ways, *and* according to the fruit of his doings.

Brothers, Sisters, and Sinners, do not for one moment think that God is asleep and does not know what we are doing. We cannot hide our secret sins from Him, for the Lord sees and knows all about us. God loves us very much, let us please Him. He is very patient with human beings; the Lord is waiting for us to come to Jesus. He wants the very best for all of us, but we must leave the wickedness of the world and ask Jesus to come into our hearts and change us.

In our hearts are lies and wickedness; therefore, we must turn to Him who can help us. It is not God's will that anyone should die and go to hell. God does not have pleasure in the suffering or death of human beings in any way, neither does He want anyone to die and go to hell. God knows that death and hell will be cast into the lake of fire, and this is not the will of God for humanity.

We human beings are at fault. We are the ones with all the problems; it is not God or His Son, Jesus. They are the ones who want to save us from our wicked ways. However, we must turn around by giving up all the things of the world that are causing us to sin against the LORD God and Jesus Christ, who is our Lord and Savior.

Believers, you said that you are a Christian, well act like one. The word Christian means Christ-like. Is your behavior like Christ in your body and life? When sin confronted Jesus, He rebuked them. Jesus worshipped the Father. Are you worshipping the Father only? Jesus bowed Himself unto the Father. Who are you bowing to? Believers, how can you say that you are a Christian, and yet you are living a life of sins and lies by doing that which is unseemly in your body? To all those who called themselves homosexual and lesbian, is this lifestyle really and truthfully of God or the devil? If this behavior causes you to die the second death, then it cannot be of God. Therefore, since this lifestyle is sinful, and if not repented of it will cause you or anyone else who committed this sin to end up in hell, then it is of the devil.

1 Corinthians 6:9-10 (KJV)

[9] Know ye not that the unrighteous shall not inherit the kingdom of God? Be not deceived: neither fornicators, nor idolaters, nor adulterers, nor effeminate, nor abusers of themselves with mankind,
[10] Nor thieves, nor covetous, nor drunkards, nor revilers, nor extortioners, shall inherit the kingdom of God.

Galatians 5:19-21 (KJV)

The scripture said,

John 3:16 (KJV)

[16] For God so loved the world, that he gave his only begotten Son, that whosoever believeth in him should not perish, but have everlasting life.

Who does not want eternal life in a glorified body? Only a foolish person will want to go to hell for eternity. God, the Father, and the Son of God, the Lord Jesus Christ, loves you very much more than any human being will ever love you. So why don't you let Him come into your life and live? Instead of letting the devil be the head of your life, why not let Jesus be the head of your life and your family?

When the sun rises in the morning from the east, what happens to the darkness? The darkness disappears. Darkness must obey the sunlight because if the dark refuses to go, then the night is more dominant than light, but darkness cannot stand light. It is the same scenario with Jesus and the devil. Jesus represents light, and the devil represents darkness. All of us before we got saved, we were in darkness, and darkness was in us, meaning that we were agents of the devil. But when we heard about the man called Jesus and we invited Him into our lives, He entered in, and the darkness that was in us fled.

Now, Jesus Christ is the only Savior that our Father in heaven sent unto us to bring light into our hearts. However, when the light of Jesus comes into us, do not for one moment think that all is well, far be it. The devil who was driven out of your life does not like it; he will try any and everything to come back into your life. It is a daily fight to stay saved because the power of darkness is very much forceful and determined to have you again, but they are not greater than the LORD God and His Son, Jesus, and the Holy Spirit that will dwell in you. OH, haven't you read or learned about the **Awesome Power** and might of God and Jesus? Well, read about what Jesus Christ did for all of those who would become God's children on the cross at Calvary.

Ephesians 1:19-23 (KJV)

19 And what *is* the exceeding greatness of his power to us-ward who believe, according to the working of his mighty power,

20 Which he wrought in Christ, when he raised him from the dead, and set *him* at his own right hand in the heavenly *places*,

21 Far above all principality, and power, and might, and dominion, and every name that is named, not only in this world, but also in that which is to come:

²² And hath put all *things* under his feet, and gave him *to be* the head over all *things* to the church,
²³ Which is his body, the fulness of him that filleth all in all.

Colossians 2:10 (KJV)
¹⁰ And ye are complete in him, which is the head of all principality and power:

All powers in high places and wickedness of both spiritual darkness and humanity's evil of heart are all subjected unto Jesus Christ, the Son of the Highest. Servants of God, to those who it pertains to, let us wait on the Lord for His anointing upon our lives and do not fake the anointing. If you have the anointing, praise the Lord, but if not, keep on living a holy life and wait on God; do not seek the anointing somewhere else. Let us stop mixing power because you want to be something that you are not before your time. Allow Jesus Christ to come in and cleanse you once again from sin. Give a place for the Spirit of God to once again use you to glorify the Son of God.

Christians, those who are living a life pleasing and acceptable unto the Lord, I honor your steadfastness in the faith. Continue to do the work of God in the name of Jesus Christ through the power and might of the Holy Spirit of God. To the unbelievers, **stop**, **listen,** and **obey** the word of God for your life. The most significant decision that you could ever make in this world is to give your life unto God and allow His Son, Christ Jesus, to wash and cleanse you from all unrighteousness. He will forgive you of your sins so that you too can have everlasting life.

Before the close of this chapter, I would like to leave the following two scripture verses with you to meditate on.

Isaiah 5:20 (KJV)
²⁰ Woe unto them that call evil good, and good evil; that put darkness for light, and light for darkness; that put bitter for sweet, and sweet for bitter!

Revelation 22:11 (KJV)

[11] He that is unjust, let him be unjust still: and he which is filthy, let him be filthy still: and he that is righteous, let him be righteous still: and he that is holy, let him be holy still.

May the Good LORD bless and keep you in every area of your life, protecting you from the attack of the enemies as you move forward in the things of God in the precious name of Jesus.

God bless and keep you. May you make the right choice by accepting Jesus as Lord and Savior of your life. Come unto Him today, for He is waiting for you right now. Yes, right where you are.

AMEN

CHAPTER ELEVEN

The Precious Blood of Jesus

What about the blood of Jesus? What is so special about the blood of Jesus Christ? What did Jesus do with His blood? Is there power in the blood of Jesus?

Genesis 9:3-4 (KJV)
3 Every moving thing that liveth shall be meat for you; even as the green herb have I given you all things.
4 But flesh with the life thereof, *which is* the blood thereof, shall ye not eat.

Leviticus 17:10-12 (KJV)
10 And whatsoever man *there be* of the house of Israel, or of the strangers that sojourn among you, that eateth any manner of blood; I will even set my face against that soul that eateth blood, and will cut him off from among his people.
11 For the life of the flesh *is* in the blood: and I have given it to you upon the altar to make an atonement for your souls: for it *is* the blood *that* maketh an atonement for the soul.
12 Therefore I said unto the children of Israel, No soul of you shall eat blood, neither shall any stranger that sojourneth among you eat blood.

Leviticus 17:14 (KJV)
14 For *it is* the life of all flesh; the blood of it *is* for the life thereof: therefore I said unto the children of Israel, Ye shall eat the blood of no

manner of flesh: for the life of all flesh *is* the blood thereof: whosoever eateth it shall be cut off.

I have come to know this for a fact that there are people in different cultures that are still eating and drinking the blood of animals. Those who are still carrying on these practices, listen to what the Bible has to say, as mentioned above. Not everything that our fore-parents or parents do is right. Many of them have done things in ignorance, not understanding what the LORD God was telling them, in all the things that are written in the Word of God, The Holy Bible.

It is evident to all those who read the scripture verses above that the blood is the life of all flesh, and because it is life, no one for any reason should eat or drink blood at any time. All those who are partaking of the consumption of blood, whether they eat or drink it, violate the word of God; it is just that simple.

Adam and Eve

When Adam and Eve were in the garden of Eden, they sinned against Jehovah God through being disobedient. What did they do? They refused to follow the instruction that God gave to them, **Genesis 2:15-17.** When they realize that they were naked, they, in turn, used fig leaves to cover themselves. Yet, the fig leaves were not sufficient to hide them from their spiritual and physical shame, so God did something better for them, which He always does, and this is how sin entered into the world - through Adam and Eve disobedient to God, the Father of all Creations. By reading the content of the word of God, we have come to realize that God uses animal skin to cover Adam and Eve, **Genesis 3:21;** therefore, we have to conclude that blood was shed in order to get the skin to cover their body. From the fall of man in the garden of Eden, God, the Father, required man's life, and since life is in the blood, the Lord God requires it so that He would not consume us because He is holy and nothing unholy is accepted in His presence.

From the garden until Jesus went to the cross, blood sacrifice was required from man to God because of human disobedient which is sin; therefore, humanity must give his life for his disobedient. But there was a "very huge" problem with mankind: we could not pay the price for our sins and be free from sin. If Adam was not qualified to pay for his wrong, neither could anyone else after Adam because of sin we cannot be qualified.

Since man could not use their blood for a blood sacrifice, that which the Lord God began in the garden continued until the perfect Lamb was available to sacrifice His life for us. The Lamb is Jesus, who is the sacrificial Lamb of the living God. Jesus came to show us the way to God, the Father, because He knows the way and He is the way. For God to forgive us for our sins, there was a need for a blood sacrifice. Only one person born of a woman was qualified to do such, and this person is Jesus Christ, who is the only begotten Son of the living God, our Father which art in heaven. That is why Jesus is the Savior of the world. No one else is pure like Him to pay for our sin, and this is why we "Christians" say that we owe the Lord our life because He gave His life for us, and by giving His life, we also inherit everlasting life with Him, never to die again. But for those who refuse Him on earth and die in their sin shall not inherit eternal life with Jesus; instead, they will have everlasting life with Satan in hell.

God's perfect will was that humanity would live forever in God's perfect Kingdom, enjoying Him and all the good that He has in store for us, but sin came, and we lost that original future with God. But it is not entirely lost because God the Father redeem us from sin by His Son Jesus Christ and reposition us for greatness in His Son Jesus Christ. Will you accept Him today so that you will have everlasting life with Jesus?

Genesis 3:7-8 (KJV)

7 And the eyes of them both were opened, and they knew that they *were* naked; and they sewed fig leaves together, and made themselves aprons.

⁸ And they heard the voice of the LORD God walking in the garden in the cool of the day: and Adam and his wife hid themselves from the presence of the LORD God amongst the trees of the garden.

Genesis 3:21 (KJV)

²¹ Unto Adam also and to his wife did the LORD God make coats of skins, and clothed them.

When Adam and Eve were in the Garden, they did not know evil. All they knew was good. They were perfect and in perfect union with their Father. That is how they were initially in the presence of God until they sinned, "disobeyed the command of God." The LORD God did not send them out of the Garden. But the scripture said that God drove them out, not only from the Garden but also from His presence. God is a holy God, and sin will not and cannot dwell in His presence. Human life was out of alignment with the Lord, and only blood could solve the problem that humans caused. Since life is in the blood, it would take blood to redeem human beings' lives from death. The blood at the beginning was just a temporarily covering and atonement for both Adam and Eve and to every human being until Jesus shed His blood for them and us. The reason why it was only temporarily is that the blood of animals cannot wash and cleanse anyone from impurity. It was not an animal that sinned. Man sinned; therefore, it will take the blood of a sinless man to pay for humanity's sin. Because humanity inherited the sin nature within themselves from the seed of our earthly first father of all the human race, Adam, all human beings are born having the sin nature in them waiting to rebel against God. That's why Jesus is the One who died for all humanity.

Every human being receives their DNA from both parent's father and mother, and man's DNA carries the sin nature and transfer it to the children. Jesus Christ DNA is not from the earth; instead, it is from heaven. Adam's DNA was from heaven because he was perfect in all sense of perfection when God created him and made him from the dust, but when he sin against the Lord, he was no longer perfect as he was created and made. But this man, Jesus, the Son of God, would inherit the sin nature from Adam if Adam was His earthly father. Since Adam was not Jesus' Father, Jesus has no sin in Him, neither did He inherit the sin nature. Therefore, Jesus's DNA is not from earthly fathers; His DNA is from His Father God. Adam was created from the dust, flesh.

According to the scripture **Luke 1:26-35,** the angel told Mary that the Holy Ghost shall come upon her, and the power of the Highest shall overshadow Mary, so she became pregnant with a man child, whose name is Jesus. So, we can now see that Jesus Christ is not earthly like Adam, who was perfect at first; but because of the devil who deceives Eve, his wife, Adam was deceived too because he became a part-taker of the fruit which he was commanded not to eat.

Remember, when Adam sinned, God used animal skin to cover their body or flesh, but the blood of that animal was not sufficient for the remission of man's sin. Why is this? Animals were not the ones that sinned, and because it was man, God required from a sinless man blood sacrifice for sin. Mankind cannot offer to God the blood sacrifice that is needed to redeem themselves from the curse of sin and the sin nature that is within them.

Humanity is not pure, we are impure; however, because we are made in the image of God, and the love that He has for us, He made it possible for us to be perfect like our fore-parents were at the beginning, Adam and Eve. Our purification from our sins can only be done through the only one who knew no sin and had no sin within Himself, and this person is Jesus, the **Savior of all.**

The blood of Jesus is pure and will never lose its power. The blood of Jesus is the only blood that can wash and cleanse us from our unrighteousness. The blood of Jesus is very much effective in our lives even now. Many Christians do not know the significance of the blood of Jesus Christ. Some Christians only have knowledge that Jesus died for their sins and that His blood was shed for their forgiveness of sins.

Yes, all of the above mentioned is true; however, He did something that many do not know that He has done: Jesus represent us to God with His blood for us on the altar in heaven.

Cane and Abel

Genesis 4:10 (KJV)
[10] And he said, What hast thou done? the voice of thy brother's blood crieth unto me from the ground.

What the Lord is saying to Cane is that his brother's innocent blood is crying out to Him for justice, and justice was served against Cane. Cane was the first murderer mentioned in the scripture. Because of jealousy, this sin nature is still very dominant in the earth today. Many are murdering one another because of jealousy. Jesus died to forgive us for this sin too.

What is so special about the Blood of Jesus Christ?

The blood of Jesus Christ is the only blood that is pure, free from the filth of sin, free of all impurity in all sense of contamination of sin, also in all aspects of filthiness. Every person that would ever be conceived of a woman is born in sin, and no matter what we do or say, we are all sinners. However, we do not have to be a sinner for the rest of our lives on this earth. We can change from a sinner to a child of God because of what Jesus did for us on the cross at Calvary. Anyone of us can be changed from a sinner to be a child of God; all we need to do is to confess our sins to God in the name of His Son Christ Jesus. The scripture said that we must believe in our hearts.

Romans 10:9-10 (KJV)
[9] That if thou shalt confess with thy mouth the Lord Jesus, and shalt believe in thine heart that God hath raised him from the dead, thou shalt be saved.

[10] For with the heart man believeth unto righteousness; and with the mouth confession is made unto salvation.

Confession is vital. Believing in what Jesus has done for us on the cross is very important for our faith. Confession is asking the Lord God to forgive you for the wrongs that you have done. Confession is telling God that you have acknowledged the sin that you have committed in your life and heart against Him, also the wrong that you have done to others. Confession is also telling Him that you are very sorry for what you have done; however, believing is very different. Some people have confessed their sins to the LORD God, yet they have not accepted all the things that the Savior of the world has done for them. Why is that? Because there is a significant disconnect between them and the LORD.

Romans 8:1 (KJV)
[1] *There is* therefore now no condemnation to them which are in Christ Jesus, who walk not after the flesh, but after the Spirit.

Not only should we confess our sins and ask God to forgive us of all unrighteousness, but the scripture is clear that we must also acknowledge who Jesus is and what God has done in and through His only begotten Son for us. To be a Christian, we must believe in our heart that Jesus died on the cross for our sins. Believe that He shed His precious blood for the remission of our sins. Believe God raised Him from the dead. The blood of Jesus Christ is the only blood that can wash, cleanse, and make all those who would come to Him vessels of honor.

Yes, when we are naturally dirty from the workplace or at home, and it could be the games that we do play, we become sweaty and dirty, some more than others. Nevertheless, all of us clean up by taking a shower, washing away the dirt that is on our bodies, and washing the dirt and sweat from our clothing. Water cleans the natural body, but only the blood of Jesus Christ can cleanse our soul from sins. Only the blood of Jesus can cover us so that our heavenly Father may have sweet communion with us. Only the blood of Jesus Christ can protect us from the enemy and help us not to live in fear, including the Holy Ghost and the angels.

No other blood, whether it is of humans or animals, birds, or whatever else it may be, will ever do for us what the blood of Jesus has already done for all those who accepted Him. The blood of Jesus gave us the victory over Satan for what He did on the cross.

We should now have a better understanding of why the blood of Jesus is so special to all the children of God. It is not just the death of Jesus Christ, the children of God throughout the world should celebrate. But we are to be so very thankful to God, the Father, for the precious blood of Jesus that was shed at Calvary. Please remember, without the shedding of blood, there is no forgiveness of our sins.

The precious blood of Jesus, which was shed for all mankind, gives us access to the throne room of God in the precious name of Jesus. No longer do we need to wait or depend upon any priest to ask the LORD God to forgive us of our sins. We, the children of God, have in heaven our High Priest Jesus, interceding on our behalf. We can go to our Father, who is in heaven at any time of the day, and speak with Him and pray to Him. God does not have an earthly communication line that will get busy when too many people are calling on Him. Christians and unbelievers know this of a truth that the heavenly communication line will never be busy when you call. Heaven is accessible twenty-four-seven, and even right now, God would like for you to call on Him in prayer. Why don't you take a moment from reading and speak to Him?

Ephesians 2:18 (KJV)

[18] For through him we both have access by one Spirit unto the Father.

Many Christians each year celebrate the death, burial, and resurrection of our Lord and Savior, Jesus Christ. That is all very good. And without His death, Christian would've experienced the second death, and there would be no hope for our salvation. However, we must be very thankful to God Almighty for the blood that His Son shed for us. We must also incorporate the shedding of Jesus' blood in our Easter celebration because the blood is vital to our redemption - **Forgiveness.**

What did Jesus do with His Blood?

To understand what Jesus did with His blood, we need to examine the Old Testament scriptures. Jehovah God had ordained and commissioned His servant, Moses, to make blood sacrifices of birds and animals and how to use the blood. All that the servant of the LORD God did under the law was an example of all that Jesus Christ, the Son of God, would come to do for us at the appointed time set forth by the Father. God has given Moses strict instruction to oversee the priestly duties that he would do it perfectly.

All that was done was exactly as commanded or perfect. Jesus Christ, the only begotten Son of God, was coming to do His priestly work here on earth as Moses and Aaron, the priest, did in the wilderness. That which was done in the Old Testament, all the sacrifices, Jesus only did it once, because once was enough. Jesus Himself became the perfect sacrificial Lamb. It would be His blood that would be shed and not that of animals or birds. So, Moses, the servant of GOD, and Aaron, the priest, was meticulous in what they were doing. We know that they have obeyed all that the LORD had asked of them to do because if they had not made the sacrifices precisely as the LORD had commanded of them to do, we would have read about their calamity. Now, let us examine what Moses did in the Old Testament and what Jesus did for us in the New Testament with His precious blood.

Exodus 12:5 (KJV)
⁵ Your lamb shall be without blemish, a male of the first year: ye shall take *it* out from the sheep, or from the goats:

Old Testament: The Lamb mentioned above is a sheep or goat. This animal to be sacrificed must be free from any kind of sickness, no spot or blemish of any kind. This lamb must be perfect. This lamb in the Old Testament sacrifice is a representation of Jesus Christ in the New Testament sacrifice to God for all humanity.

New Testament: Please examine the scripture above very carefully; Jesus Christ is the Lamb of God who has no blemishes. He never sinned, nor knew any sin. He was the One who was chosen to be the perfect sacrifice for the sins of all humanity because He has no sin in Him.

1 Peter 2:24 (KJV)
24 Who his own self bare our sins in his own body on the tree, that we, being dead to sins, should live unto righteousness: by whose stripes ye were healed.

With confidence, we can say before we get saved, we are like goats in our behavior and conduct; therefore, God chose Jesus of all the sheep and goats. We know that Jesus was like a sheep in His manner and characteristics. Jesus did not open His mouth or complain. He took up the cross, knowing the death that He will have to go through. Jesus was humble unto His death, in all fullness of obedience to His Father, to be the perfect sacrifice for all humanity.

Exodus 12:7 (KJV)
7 And they shall take of the blood, and strike *it* on the two side posts and on the upper door post of the houses, wherein they shall eat it.

Some people mistakenly used the word spill, referring to the blood of Jesus. The blood of Jesus Christ was not spilled, when something spill it is an accident; but rather, His blood was shed; there is a vast difference. The blood of Jesus sprinkled upon the doorpost of all believers' hearts by His Spirit. Now we can live a life of peace, knowing that we, the children of God, are currently under Divine protection from on High because of the blood of Jesus.

Exodus 12:13 (KJV)

[13] And the blood shall be to you for a token upon the houses where ye *are*: and when I see the blood, I will pass over you, and the plague shall not be upon you to destroy *you*, when I smite the land of Egypt.

The blood gives us protection from the enemy of death. The LORD God made a promise to His children, the righteous ones, that they will be protected as long as the blood of Jesus is sprinkled upon their hearts; when danger comes by our home, it will pass over us because of the blood.

We must be cautious about how we live our life after we asked Jesus to come into our hearts to be Lord and Savior. Why? Even though we are Christians, we can step out of the will of God, and the devil can and will have the right to harm us because we have allowed him into our lives once again. When we find ourselves out of the will of God, we must repent immediately and get back into the right relationship with God.

The children of righteousness are not purchased with money, but with the precious blood and the life of Jesus Christ only, and that's it. We are blood-bought, blood-washed from all unrighteousness with the precious blood of Jesus. Yes, it is because of the blood that we are protected from the wrath of God, both present and future. When God looked upon us, His children, He does not see us as sinners. He sees us as vessels of honor without spot and wrinkles all because of Jesus. This is the Church that Jesus dies for and is coming back for, the spiritual church, which is the Saints. We are cleansed from unrighteousness to righteousness, by the sprinkling of Jesus' blood upon all those who accepted Him as the Son of God and their Lord and Savior.

Exodus 12:21-22 (KJV)

[21] Then Moses called for all the elders of Israel, and said unto them, Draw out and take you a lamb according to your families, and kill the passover.

²² And ye shall take a bunch of hyssop, and dip *it* in the blood that *is* in the bason, and strike the lintel and the two side posts with the blood that *is* in the bason; and none of you shall go out at the door of his house until the morning.

The very same thing happened to Jesus when He entered Jerusalem before the Passover to be killed. He was chosen out by the priest in those days to be the One who they would crucify. They would rather crucify Jesus, the humble One, and save the one whose lifestyle and manner is like a goat. Between Jesus and Barabbas, they choose the humble and perfect One to be crucified instead of the ungodly.

Matthew 27:17 (KJV)

¹⁷ Therefore when they were gathered together, Pilate said unto them, Whom will ye that I release unto you? Barabbas, or Jesus which is called Christ?

Matthew 27:20 (KJV)

²⁰ But the chief priests and elders persuaded the multitude that they should ask Barabbas, and destroy Jesus.

Matthew 27:22-23 (KJV)

²² Pilate saith unto them, What shall I do then with Jesus which is called Christ? *They* all say unto him, Let him be crucified.
²³ And the governor said, Why, what evil hath he done? But they cried out the more, saying, Let him be crucified.

Even Pilate, the ungodly ruler, did not find any fault in Jesus, but the religious people who are supposed to know better wanted Jesus to be crucified. Well, this is the problem even now! Many church people are religious, and that's all they are. When they are supposed to have the salvation experience from God by His Son and become spiritual. God already knew the wickedness in the hearts of those religious people; therefore, He chose this death for His only begotten Son. Please remember this, even though the suffering and death of Jesus Christ was terrifying and horrible in the sense of what they did to Him, it was a man who sinned in the Garden of Eden. It would take a sinless man to pay for our sins, and Jesus became the sacrificial Lamb.

Humanity could never pay for their sins because we are not worthy of paying the cost that is required of us; only Jesus Christ, the Lamb of God, who knew no sin, and in Him, there was no guile; therefore, He was the One that was chosen to pay for all of humanity's sins. This is why unbelievers and Christians must be so joyful in thanksgiving unto God and our Lord and Savior, Jesus Christ, because of what He has done for us on Calvary. If Jesus did not die and shed His blood for us, there would be no hope for us to have a heavenly relationship with our heavenly Father. All of us would be lost forever, but thanks be to Jesus, who made it possible for us to come back or reconcile us to our Father.

Exodus 24:6-8 (KJV)
[6] And Moses took half of the blood, and put *it* in basons; and half of the blood he sprinkled on the altar.
[7] And he took the book of the covenant, and read in the audience of the people: and they said, All that the LORD hath said will we do, and be obedient.
[8] And Moses took the blood, and sprinkled *it* on the people, and said, Behold the blood of the covenant, which the LORD hath made with you concerning all these words.

Here we see that Moses took half of the blood and sprinkled it on the altar, and then he sprinkled it on the book and the people, thus sealing the covenant that God made with the people. We know that Jesus sprinkled His blood upon our heart and also on the altar, sealing the New Testament covenant in His blood. The blood of Jesus gave us access to God, our heavenly Father, who is also the Father of our Lord and Savior, Jesus Christ. We know that there is an altar in heaven because the scripture mentions it.

Revelation 8:3 (KJV)
³ And another angel came and stood at the altar, having a golden censer; and there was given unto him much incense, that he should offer *it* with the prayers of all saints upon the golden altar which was before the throne.

Jesus represent us with His blood on the altar in heaven for all those who would come to worship the only true GOD in the entire Universe. One day, those that rejected God's Son will eventually acknowledge Him as the only begotten Son of God, and you will bow and worship His Majesty.

Exodus 29:16 (KJV)
¹⁶ And thou shalt slay the ram, and thou shalt take his blood, and sprinkle *it* round about upon the altar.

Leviticus 3:8 (KJV)
⁸ And he shall lay his hand upon the head of his offering, and kill it before the tabernacle of the congregation: and Aaron's sons shall sprinkle the blood thereof round about upon the altar.

Now we have a much clearer understanding of what Jesus did with His blood, and why it is not just about His death, it is also about His precious blood that was shed for all humanity. The sad thing is many people in this world do not believe that Jesus is the Son of God. Even some Christians do not believe that God and Jesus are two separate persons. Jesus Christ is the only begotten of the Father, full of grace and truth, who sits on the right hand of God the Father.

Hebrew 1:1-3
Psalms 110:1 (KJV)
¹ The LORD said unto my Lord, Sit thou at my right hand, until I make thine enemies thy footstool.

Thanksgivings to God and Jesus

Lord Jesus, we love you very much with all of our heart, we adore you, and we exalt you above every other name on the earth. Lord Jesus, among humanity, no name is so precious like yours. We thank you for coming unto humanity to give your life so that we as human beings can once again have a relationship with our dear heavenly Father, GOD. We know that God has reconciled us through your death and blood to Himself, who is our heavenly Father.

Father God, thank you for your Son, Jesus. Knowing the death that He would experience, the suffering in agony for the sins. He died once, never to die again, and now He lives forevermore. Because He lives forevermore; likewise, we who die in righteousness will be liked unto Jesus, that after our physical death, we too will never die again and will live forevermore. Oh, Lord God, our Father, we thank you! Father, there is so much to be thankful for; you are wonderful, kind, and faithful to humanity. We thank you for all the miraculous things that you have done for us, both in our spiritual and physical lives.

Father God, we appreciate you so much that there are no words that we can come up with to express our gratitude to you. We thank you for your Holy Spirit. Forever, we will say this by giving you the highest praise – Hallelujah, hallelujah to you, Father God. Thank you very, very much in your Son precious name! Jesus. ***Amen***

Is there power in the Blood?

Oh yes, there is power in the blood of the Lamb, wonder-working power in the blood of Jesus Christ. The blood of Jesus Christ washes all of God's children, both those in the Old Testament and the New Testament, reconciling all to God and all those who accepted His Son, Christ Jesus.

Is there power in the blood of Jesus? Oh, yes, it consecrates all unbelievers to become believers from the filthiness of sin, which is unrighteousness. Because of the blood of Jesus, Father God can now look upon all those who have accepted His Son, Jesus, as if they have no sin. God looks at them, and all He sees is the blood wash, blood brought children of the Highest.

Yes, there is so much power in the blood of Jesus. The blood of Jesus frees all who need to be loosed from the grip of sin. The blood of Jesus is not only a protection for Christians, but it also protects our loved ones. When we do pray and ask Father God to cover them with the blood of Jesus, they received protection over their unsaved lives.

The blood of Jesus Christ is so powerful that during the time of His death and resurrection, some believers who were dead and buried rose from the graves. How could Jesus die one place and yet Saints that were buried in different areas rose from the dead? I have told you that there is power in the blood of the Lamb of God, and the Lamb of God is Jesus.

Know this, the resurrection of Jesus Christ gives humanity hope and to the Saints after death; those that died and the ones that are alive in righteousness will also be resurrected like Him at His first coming. At the first coming, the dead in unrighteousness will not be resurrected to life, but there is a day coming when the unrighteous will come alive to face their sentence for refusing the gift of God, His Son, Jesus Christ, and the eternal life that is in Him. Rapture means: "Jesus comes and takes away the righteous people from among the unrighteous." It was the application of His precious blood that was shed that completed the work. The death of Jesus and the shedding of His blood, Jesus did something for us that no man in the entire Universe could ever do for us, neither will there be one to come.

Matthew 27:52-53 (KJV)
[52] And the graves were opened; and many bodies of the saints which slept arose,

[53] And came out of the graves after his resurrection, and went into the holy city, and appeared unto many.

Jesus did not shed His blood for naught. Oh no, the blood of Jesus sealed all the Old Testament Saint's redemption because they are now in heaven. Not only them, but every New Testament Saint will be with the Lord. Even us who are alive now and are washed with the precious blood of Jesus, we too will be in heaven with the Lord.

Hebrews 9:12 (KJV)
[12] Neither by the blood of goats and calves, but by his own blood he entered in once into the holy place, having obtained eternal redemption *for us.*

Hebrews 9:14 (KJV)
[14] How much more shall the blood of Christ, who through the eternal Spirit offered himself without spot to God, purge your conscience from dead works to serve the living God?

Hebrews 9:24 (KJV)
[24] For Christ is not entered into the holy places made with hands, *which are* the figures of the true; but into heaven itself, now to appear in the presence of God for us:

Jesus Christ, our High Priest, entered into the holy of holies only once for us. Now, we, the children of the only true living God, can enter into the holy of holies for ourselves as many times as we desire to receive from our Father mercy and forgiveness. Jesus went and presented Himself for us as the high priest did in the Old Testament, offering sacrifices for the people once a year; Jesus only has to do it once. He was the perfect sacrifice without blemish, and His sacrifice was accepted by God only once.

There are many Christians who are living their Christian life in condemnation; why is that? Some of us have not yet perfected our faith in the work that the Son of God did for them on the cross at Calvary. Many have allowed other Christians, their brothers and sisters, or maybe even their pastors, to condemn them. They believe that they are not truly saved by the death and shed blood of Jesus. Please get up from where you fall in the mighty name of Jesus Christ and repent to God in Jesus' name and move on in righteousness unto eternal life, which is in Jesus.

The Bible says:

Romans 8:1 (KJV)
[1] *There is* therefore now no condemnation to them which are in Christ Jesus, who walk not after the flesh, but after the Spirit.

Yes, if your Christian life is after the flesh, you are already condemned if you do not change; read the scripture very carefully. However, if you are living your life by the Spirit, no one has the right to condemn you in any manner because Jesus did not come to condemn us but to save us from sin. Christian's lives **must** line up according to the word of God in their lives, and we must bear good fruit!

Matthew 7:20 (KJV)
[20] Wherefore by their fruits ye shall know them.

At no time should we, as Christians, allow the devil to enter into our lives and cause us to disgrace the name of Jesus Christ. We have to be very careful in the words that we speak and the things that we do. The world is watching Christians if we are what we claim to be. The fruit that is bearing in our lives must be good fruit and not corrupt fruit like unto the unbelievers. All Christians are children of the only and true Holy Father who is in heaven. Our Father in heaven is so holy and pure that these words cannot compliment Jehovah God in His Sovereignty. God is so holy that everything in heaven—yes, everything in heaven! —where God dwells is pure, **Amen.**

Therefore, children, our heavenly Father is the only true GOD throughout the entire Universe. He is the Highest and He represents good. Through the power of His Holy Spirit, in the name of His Son, Christ Jesus, God almighty has called us to be holy. Let us examine ourselves and see which areas in our lives need to be changed. We must make these changes immediately so that we can please God and not man. What? Christians, do we think that God sent His only begotten Son to this world to suffer and die for our sins and shed His precious blood for the remission of our sins so that we can live in unrighteousness? God forbids.

The blood of Jesus Christ that was shed for us must mean something. Many of us think that we can be a Christian and still do the things of unrighteousness. Should we continue to sin as if we were not bought with a precious price? God forbids. Jesus gave His life for us and His blood was shed, whether we like it or not. Know this, that which Jesus did for humanity on the cross will never be changed by anyone of us. The words of God are a witness to the glorious and graceful act of our Lord and Savior, Jesus Christ.

Revelation 12:10-11 (KJV)

[10] And I heard a loud voice saying in heaven, Now is come salvation, and strength, and the kingdom of our God, and the power of his Christ: for the accuser of our brethren is cast down, which accused them before our God day and night.
[11] And they overcame him by the blood of the Lamb, and by the word of their testimony; and they loved not their lives unto the death.

Believers, the scripture tells us this, that by the blood of the Lamb and our testimony, we overcome. We in the Christian community must include our celebrations of the death of Jesus with His shed blood for all of us. There is not enough emphasis anymore in the Churches of God about the blood of Jesus Christ and its meaning. If we don't start preaching again, the blood that was shed for us in power and might under the anointed power of the Holy Ghost we'll lose its fire. Pastors, it's time to go back to the old-time preaching, that is we must inform God's children about the death and shed blood of His Son.

Ephesians 1:7 (KJV)

⁷ In whom we have redemption through his blood, the forgiveness of sins, according to the riches of his grace;

Acts 20:28 (KJV)

²⁸ Take heed therefore unto yourselves, and to all the flock, over the which the Holy Ghost hath made you overseers, to feed the church of God, which he hath purchased with his own blood.

1 John 1:7 (KJV)

⁷ But if we walk in the light, as he is in the light, we have fellowship one with another, and the blood of Jesus Christ his Son cleanseth us from all sin.

Hebrews 10:19 (KJV)

¹⁹ Having therefore, brethren, boldness to enter into the holiest by the blood of Jesus,

Hebrews 10:29 (KJV)

²⁹ Of how much sorer punishment, suppose ye, shall he be thought worthy, who hath trodden underfoot the Son of God, and hath counted the blood of the covenant, wherewith he was sanctified, an unholy thing, and hath done despite unto the Spirit of grace?

Saints, there is power in the blood of Jesus. If there were no power in His blood, all our hope of redemption is lost. There would be no reason for anyone of us to pursue the righteousness of God. All that Jesus did for us would be in vain. However, we know by faith that all of our righteousness through the death and shed blood of Jesus on the cross was and still is perfect and true, knowing all those that would boldly come to Him by faith will be saved.

Every human being is a child of God. However, not all of His children are living in righteousness. There is no color barrier among Christians and should never be. We are looked upon by the Almighty God as His people. There should be no discrimination at all in our Christian life. By the way, which God are we serving? We are not serving a God that hates people. Haven't we been reading the Bible about the love that the Father has for us that He gave us His only begotten Son?

Yes, we are all children of God; however, there are good children and bad children, but we are all His children. The same in our family, there are good children and bad children, yet they are all family. The difference between God's children on this earth is that all good children are not referred to as just doing good works because good works alone will not save anyone. However, it is those who truly come to accept Jesus Christ as their personal Savior. Those that are considered bad children are those who rejected Jesus Christ, the Son of God. They are the ones who live their lives in disobedience to the word of God. All those who reject Christ have also rejected God, the Father, who has sent unto us His dear son, Jesus Christ.

Yes, some of us rejected God, the Father of Jesus, because they believed only in Jesus Christ, the Son. Yes, some of us believe in Jesus Christ and not the God the Father, because they think that the Father and the Son are the same. Yes, if you have accepted Jesus Christ, the Son, you have also accepted the Father who has sent the Son; however, if any person rejected the Son of God, they have rejected the Father who sent the Son according to the scripture.

Why is this? Because that person has not believed that the Son came forth from the Father and did the works that He had done. Jesus did not come to do His will, but rather, Jesus came to do the will of the Father who sent Him.

The blood that Jesus shed on the cross was for all humanity throughout the four corners of the earth; it was not for animals or angels. They do not need a blood sacrifice to save them from the wrath to come. All human beings upon the face of the earth need someone to sacrifice their life for humanity in order to save them from their sins, but this blood sacrifice could only come from the Son of God. The precious blood of Jesus washes us and cleanses us from all unrighteousness, giving all of God's children access to the throne room where we can enter in and receive mercy and forgiveness, including direction for our lives. Only the blood of Jesus can cleanse us, and despite what some may say, there is no other blood that can do for us what the blood of Jesus does for all mankind.

Whether we believe it or not, nothing will change what the word of God said. Jesus is the only begotten Son of God, and He is the One who came to be our sacrificial Lamb. This sacrifice was done through His death and shed blood on the cross at Calvary.

Yes, believers, there is an unlimited source of power in the blood of Jesus Christ. The blood of Jesus is the atonement for our sins. Therefore, to everyone who is called children of the living God in Christ Jesus, hold fast to your faith of the cross. The work that Jesus did for us has given us victory over death and the grave. It does get rough sometimes, but don't ever give up, because if we miss heaven, we will miss it all.

To God be the Glory,
Amen.

ABOUT THE AUTHOR

Pastor Denburk Gregory

I was born in Manchester, Jamaica, West Indies. I grew up with my grandmother, Sister Vera Thomas. At a young age, my grandmother told me many times that one day I would be like the Reverend Billy Graham. I grew up with my twin brother and sister in a Christian home. I am the first boy of five boys and two sisters.

Every Sunday morning, we would walk to church about three miles, and most Sunday nights, we would repeat the same for night service. There was no smoking or drinking of alcohol in my grandmother's home because she was a saved grandmother, and even now I cannot tolerate alcohol in my body, neither do I smoke.

My parents, Mr. Stanford and Ms. Esmie (Daddy & Mommy), left us in Jamaica and moved to England, Great Britain, leaving us with our grandmother so that they can make a better life for themselves and us their children. I must say that they have indeed taken care of us as parents. Thank God that our mother is still alive. Since this book was written some years ago, my father has passed away. God bless you, mommy, and daddy rest in peace.

In Jamaica, I attended the New Broughton Secondary School until graduation. One of my favorite sports while in school was track and field. My brother, sister, and I were the fastest runners while we were attending school.

On October 10, 1975, we came to the United States of America to be with our father and mom. I lived in Brooklyn, New York, for twenty-seven years. While in New York, I worked for a company name White Castle System, Inc., for twenty- five years as a store manager in several different locations. I truly enjoyed the time spent there, and I wish there was a store in the South of the country where my family and I moved to; if there was, I would still be working for them.

In 2002, my family and I moved from New York to reside in Cumming, Georgia. The Lord has taken me from Jamaica to New York, and then to Georgia, to fulfill the prophecy that my grandmother did prophecy over my life as a young child. While attending a church in Cumming, I went through training as the Lord would have it. I was in leadership training for a while, and after a period of training under the guidance of my Pastors, Apostle David, and Joyce Smith, the Holy Ghost had them ordain me as a pastor. I am now a pastor in the Full Truth Church of God Deliverance Center, for now, we only have one church here.

I am very thankful to the Lord for all that He has done for my family and me. The Lord has a way of bringing things together even though the time may seem long; it will happen so that His perfect will come to pass. One of the final parts of my life is that I have found a woman, Veronica, who is my wife, she loves the Lord Jesus Christ, and that's make my life much easier to live. This is my story for now, God bless each of you out there.

To God be the glory, Amen

www.ingramcontent.com/pod-product-compliance
Lightning Source LLC
Chambersburg PA
CBHW071624030726
47598CB00001B/420